The Stock Market Bubble Bust Of 2015 And Beyond

The Stock Market Bubble Bust Of 2015 And Beyond

Michael Swanson

ISBN: 1517186323
ISBN 13: 9781517186326

TABLE OF CONTENTS

Introduction · vii

Chapter 1 A New Bear Market Is Here · · · · · · · · · · · · · · 1

Chapter 2 Three Signs of a Top · · · · · · · · · · · · · · · · · 11

Chapter 3 Managing Risk In A Bear Market· · · · · · · · · · 24

Chapter 4 How to Buy During a Bear Market · · · · · · · · 41

Chapter 5 The Debt Danger and Gold · · · · · · · · · · · · · 54

Chapter 6 How To Profit From A Gold Bull Market · · · · 77

Afterword · 93

Acknowledgements · · · · · · · · · · · · · · · · · · · 95

About the Author· 97

INTRODUCTION

I am glad you bought this book and opened it up, because I believe that we are at a critical moment in the financial markets that will impact our investments for years. In fact right now we may have seen the S&P 500 and the United States stock market recently peak at such a high valuation level that it may not be surpassed again for decades. I decided to write this book for you to warn you of what of I think is to come and why. And I hope to help you to prepare, to adapt, and to adjust to these new emerging market trends that are just starting. It is at the beginning of September, 2015 as I submit this book to the publisher. I hope to have this book out as quickly as I can, because I truly believe that time is of the essence. The stock market has already tipped into a bear market and I fear that we may be facing a serious stock market decline before this year is over, and probably in October or November.

Now the DOW Jones Industrial average topped out this year on May 20, 2015, when it hit an intraday high of 18,350.

The S&P 500 also made a peak that day at 2,134.71. The S&P 500 then got back up near this level again in July, but lost momentum right as it approached it. At the same time the Nasdaq made a major top on July 20, 2015, when it hit an intraday high of 5,231.

I believe the market averages have topped for good this year and already started a new bear market last month. This may seem like a bold statement to make, because the dominant opinion in the financial media is that we are seeing a normal correction and "everything is fine" with the US economy so there is no reason for the stock market to drop. And what is more, although earnings reports have been weak so far this year, most Wall Street analysts are still calling for a big earnings explosion to drive stock prices higher by the end of the year.

If you had listened to such bullish talk from the "experts" though back in 2007 and 2000 you would have lost a lot of money when the market went into a bear market. The reality is the stock market moves in cycles and bear markets are just a part of investing. Many have forgotten this, because all of the dips we have seen in the past few years have turned into buying opportunities.

Most people right now simply see very little risk in the stock market. So many have seemingly convinced themselves that the stock market is simply going to go up forever when bear markets are actually a common occurrence. If you define a bear market as a stock market drop of a least 20% there have been 29 of them since 1929. Now on average these bear markets have resulted in a decline of over 35% and have lasted for ten months. But some have been worse. The last bear market that resulted in the crash of 2008 brought with it a drop of over 65% for the S&P 500 and there are a lot of reasons to think that this new bear market is going to end up being one of the bad ones.

But the market has not fallen enough to make people really worry about it yet. So you may be wondering why should you think the stock market will drop now?

First let me tell you who I am. If you do not know already, I run a financial website called WallStreetWindow.com and operate a small private group on it called Power Investor. I have been warning about a potential top in the stock market for well over a year and told people that there were clear signs that the top was about to come in July. At the end of that month in the Power Investor group I actually took short positions to bet against the stock market in my model rebalancing portfolio. Now I notify members of the group when I make changes to that portfolio. Much of the writings in this book are from articles I have written over the past few months on my website and elsewhere on the internet. This book is a polished compendium of these articles to give you what I believe are the most critical things you need to know now to understand what is happening with the stock market and how to navigate things over the next few years. These articles also were first shared with my private group over the past few months before the stock market broke down in the last week of August, but enough time has now passed that they can be distributed to the general public.

If you want to know more about me and find out what I have to say going forward then you should go to my website WallStreetWindow.com.

From 2003 to 2006 I co-managed a hedge fund that generated a return of over 78% during that time frame and in one year was ranked in the top 35 funds out of over 5,000 tracked by performance by hedgefund.net. I'm not perfect, though. In the first year of the fund's existence I barely made anything even though the stock market went up a lot. I made a killing in the 2008 market crash personally betting against stocks but didn't adjust to the new bull market in 2009 until a few months after the bottom. I got into gold in 2002 and made a lot of money in the gold market from trading it until 2007. Then last year I bought gold and mining stocks early and took some hits in them. But right now I still hold some positions in these type of investments as I believe they will end up going up huge with what is to come. I just got in early.

But what is important for you is that I have had some of my best years making money in the stock market during the last two bear markets by betting against the stock market and even individual stocks. I was able to identify those tops in the stock market and adjust to them and the same things that happened as those bear markets just started have begun to happen again. This has dire ramifications for those that do not adjust to the markets now. Let me show you why I am convinced that this is now the case in this book and show you what you can do about it.

CHAPTER 1

A NEW BEAR MARKET IS HERE

There are three things that occur to mark a major top in the stock market and all of them have been put in place over the past few months. First of all you need to understand that all financial markets move in cycles that repeat again and again. People tend to think that news drives the markets, but it is really the other way around in that interpretations of financial news tends to match the feelings people have of the markets. So at bull market tops just about everyone interprets all financial news as supportive of higher prices and at bear market bottoms it seems that bad times will never end. News reporters spin their news accordingly, because the sources they talk to reflect the mass psychology of the markets.

So you must understand financial cycles and not chase news reports in order to understand exactly what type of market environment you are in and to adapt to it. Each cycle requires a different type of trading and investing. If you try to hold during a bear market you will lose money and if you try to bet against stocks during a bull market you will lose money too. There is no reason to fear a bear market. Bear markets are simply a part of market cycles just as winter is one of the four seasons that you experience every year. Bear market are inevitable. They have not been abolished by the Federal Reserve. If anything the policies of the Federal Reserve over the past decade have guaranteed that the next bear market is going to be a disaster.

What you need to know is that all financial markets move in bull and bear cycles that typically last three to five years. These are also in between periods between their bull and bear cycles. That makes for four cycles that you need to be aware of and to be able to recognize in order to understand the big picture of what is happening in any financial market with total clarity.

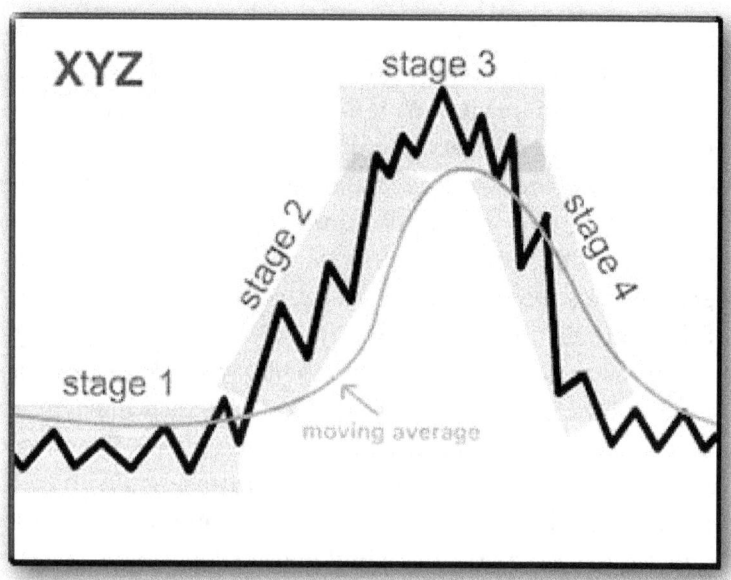

I call these cycles the four stages of a financial market. A stage one market comes after a bear market decline. It is characterized mainly by sideways price activity. It can last a few weeks and often goes on for months. Sometimes it can even go on for over a year. During a stage one market most people are actually negative about the market, because they have been brainwashed by the bear market that came before to be scared of the market. If they owned positions during the preceding bear market they suffered so much pain that they simply do not want to feel anymore. Most people who managed to hold on in the last bear market end up selling during the stage one sideways basing market.

Stocks in a stage one basing market are often at a super low valuation level that does attract the few real fundamental investors that do exist in the market. These are the people who really know what they are doing. They buy, because things are cheap and they are willing to hold and wait for the market to recognize what they know even if it takes time. Industry insiders often buy during a stage one base, because they are able to recognize that some sort of bottom is going on in their industry. If you look at insider buying and selling data you often will find that it is during a stage one basing phase that most insider purchases take place.

However, stocks and markets in a stage one base tend to go nowhere but sideways. When they go up they have rallies that don't last and when they go down they tend to just fall and bounce back up. The temporary pullbacks, though, scare people into selling for fear of another bear market. Stage one bases fool the masses.

The reason why stocks and markets in a stage one base go sideways so much is that in the end what drives financial markets are the forces of supply and demand and nothing else. Bull markets are not created because of good news. In fact there are times when the news is good and markets fall anyway.

And, there are times when the news is bad that make for great investment buy points. Most people do nothing, though, but pay attention to the news in order to understand the reasons why a market moves even though the news is totally useless when it comes to understanding the big picture and changes in stock market cycles. What you need to understand is what really moves prices. Markets move in price trends created by the forces of supply and demand. Things are as simple as that.

Bull markets go up when there are more buyers than sellers in a market and bear markets go down when there are more sellers than buyers. In a stage one base the forces of buying and selling are actually roughly equal, which is why prices go sideways. This is what creates a stage one base.

A stage one base comes to an end when the number of buyers in a market overtakes the number of sellers. Typically, you can look at a stock chart in a stage one base and identify a resistance level that has acted as a lid on prices for some time. It is a level that has attracted sellers again and again, and has stopped rallies. When the stage one base ends this level gets smashed as the sellers liquidate their final shares. Then a new bull market begins.

The best time to invest in a market is at the end of a stage one base. The next best time is in the first few months of a new bull market. During a new bull market the buyers are in control and are able to keep bidding a market up. There are pullbacks during a bull market as some sell into rallies and many trade in and out, but such pullbacks make for great buying opportunities. Most of the gains in a stage two market actually come in the first year of a bull market. That makes getting in early really important.

As a bull market continues after the first year, more and more people get excited about the market and get in. But in the end, there is a limit to how many people and how much money there is out there to get into a market. Once that limit is reached a market will enter a stage three topping phase. Then it will begin to go sideways and many of the stocks inside the market lose momentum and turn down. Money goes into fewer and fewer stocks as a real problem with liquidity begins to emerge. However, most people are incredibly bullish during a topping market, because their brains have been programmed by the bull market moves of the past to believe the market is going to go up forever. They are also fully invested at the top so they look for reasons to convince themselves that the market is going to go higher for them.

Stocks get expensive in a stage three topping market, but the masses don't care. Insiders sell out to take advantage of the high valuations that the masses are now willing to pay to get in stocks. All the masses care about is that stocks have gone up and may go up more. They become willing to pay any price to get in due to their greed for more gains or simple fear of missing out while someone else could possibly make money without them.

When the masses complete their buying there is literally no longer enough buyers in the market to keep it going up.

Then the sellers take over and send the market into a new bear market. As the market rolls over, the masses fail to realize what is going on, because they have been so brainwashed by the last bull market to see every dip as a buying opportunity. They were in the bull market, but they no longer are. Now rallies represent traps. The dumb money gets eaten alive by bear attacks.

The longer a bear market goes on the more pain people feel in it. The growing pain makes more and more people sell. Once someone sells, they become bearish on a market. As a bear market ends there is often a selling climax of panic as people dump their remaining stocks at once in fear and disgust. After a bear market, people who managed to hold on continue to sell in the stage one basing phase in disappointment, impatience, and simple fear whenever a pullback in the sideways base occurs.

These cycles repeat again and again and will never go away. They have existed throughout financial history and are created by human nature. If you can understand these cycles, recognize them, and act on that knowledge, you can make money in the financial markets by buying and selling at the best times possible and while avoiding the bear markets that hurt so many. You will then separate yourself from the masses and become a super investor.

It's all about making your investing decisions based on principles grounded in the reality of the iron laws of human nature instead of the delusions of the crowd. The good news is that it is easy to recognize these cycles if you use some basic technical indicators that you can find in any stock market charting program or website. They are the long-term 200 and 150-day moving averages.

A moving average is calculated by adding up all of the price points in a given time period and dividing that time period by the number of days in it. So a 200-day moving average is the average price of a stock or market in the past 200 days. The 150-day moving average is the average price over the past 150 days, and so on.

The 200-day and 150-day moving averages, when plotted out on a chart, give you a simple way to recognize the overall price trend you are looking at. During a bull market these moving averages go up and tend to actually act as a support level buy point during the occasional dips and corrections that occur from time to time in a bull market. At the same time, during a bear market they curl down on the chart and move down to act as resistance areas that cap rallies in bear markets.

After a bear market, these moving averages go sideways in a stage one base. This means that you can easily recognize what stage a market is in by looking at these moving averages. It also means that you can tell when a market is in a stage one base after a bear market, which makes for a great time to make some long-term investments. Investing at the start of a bull market is great as well, and being cautious after a bull market has gone on for a long-time or is actually in a bear market is prudent too. When you make investment decisions in alignment with these big trends you master the market. This is your key to the kingdom.

I talk about this concept in great detail in my previous book, Strategic Stock Trading, but take a look at the S&P 500 for the past twenty years to see how this plays out for yourself.

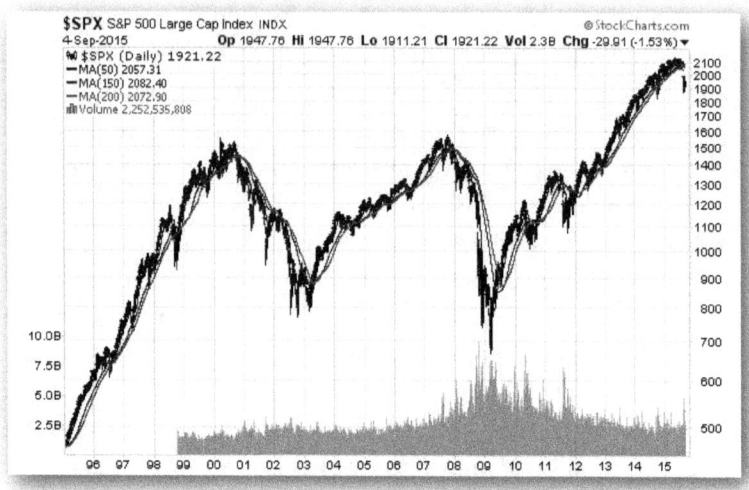

There was a little recession in the American economy during the Presidency of George H.W. Bush that caused a little bear market for the United States (US) stock market in the early 1990's and then a subsequent stage one basing phase that caused a lot of people to get out of the stock market. Once that stage one sideways basing phase ended in 1995, the S&P 500 began a giant stage two bull market that came to an end in 2000. It then went through a stage three topping market that came to an end in the fall of that year

After that the S&P 500 began a vicious stage four bear market that took prices to a bottom in 2002. Then the US stock market went through a stage one sideways basing phase that ended in 2003. A new bull market then began that lasted until 2007. Next, a short-lived stage three topping phase occurred once again that marked a transition period into a new bear market and the financial crash of 2008.

Now if you go back and look carefully at the chart of the S&P 500 you just saw you will notice that I have placed the 150 and 200-day moving averages on it. If you study this carefully you'll see what they did during all of these different market stages. As you discover the pattern you will see how clearly they act during a stage two bull market and a stage four bear market.

Look carefully and you will see that in a bull market these moving averages point up and rise. They also tend to act as support buy points for the occasional corrections that occur during a bull market. As a bull market comes to an end these moving averages tend to stop going up and spend a few months going sideways during a stage three topping phase.

During bear markets, these moving averages slope down and move down. In bear markets, the sellers are in control and send the market lower. The stock market makes lower lows and lower highs in a bear market. Rallies that are counter to the bear trend tend to come to an end at the long-term 150 and 200-day moving averages. So these averages act as tough resistance during stage four bear markets. If you held in the bear market of 2008 or after the 2000 top you probably would have done better for yourself if you had known all of this back then.

As a bear market comes to an end, though, the rate of decline in the moving averages tends to slow down. Once a bear market ends you get a stage one basing phase that acts as a transition period into a new bull market. During a stage one basing phase the moving averages bottom out and go sideways. Stage one basing phases can last a few months or even a year in duration. If you go and take the time to look at other markets you will see the same patterns repeat again and again.

This year the S&P 500, DOW, and Nasdaq all completed stage three tops. The DOW and the S&P 500 actually topped out before the Nasdaq did. But the S&P 500 held above its 200-day moving average until August 21, 2015. On that day the S&P 500 closed below this key technical level and collapsed to begin a full blown stage four bear market that is still continuing to this day. This is not a normal correction as many are saying it is as I write this. In order to understand why I say this you have to understand what led up to this big drop.

CHAPTER 2

THREE SIGNS OF A TOP

T here are three major things that happen to bring a top in the stock market. The first is that people get wildly bullish on the market to the point that people in the stock market come to believe that they risk nothing by being in the market and can only risk missing out if they are no longer fully invested. Many turn themselves into margin maniacs out of greed. So the first thing you see to bring in an important market top is manic bullish psychology. The second thing you see are very high stock valuations and the final and most important thing you see is a breakdown in the internal stock market structure. Let's look at psychology first as we examine the three signs of a top together.

Now, there is one important thing you must know about bull and bear cycles in financial markets. Although you can easily identify what cycle a market is in by applying stage analysis to a chart, very few people know how to do this. And, even those who know how to use it tend not to apply it, because to use stage analysis requires going against the crowd at critical moments in the financial markets and human psychology makes it difficult for people to do this. To go against the crowd means to face the possible rejection by a person's peers. Most conform to fit in. In many parts of your life it is beneficial for you to fit in and conform, but not when it comes to investing.

The masses look at nothing and know nothing when it comes to investing. All they do is react to the news and the price movements of the past six months and expect them to go on forever. That's why so many of them sell out on bottoms and buy on tops again and again, and never seem to learn. Most are simply incapable of investing at the end of a bear market or at the start of a new bull market, because everyone they know is being negative about investing too. What is worse, usually the TV news says the market is bad after bear market bottoms and it's hard for people to go against what they see and hear on their television sets.

The psychology behind the market has a lot to do with people's perceptions of the market. According to various services that poll investors and advisers, such as Investors Intelligence, most investors are wildly bullish at the tops of bull markets and totally bearish at a bottom, which means most people are always thinking and doing the wrong thing at key points in the cycle of a market. This is why so many buy at tops and sell on bottoms over and over again.

The reason why is that bear markets are driven by selling. As long as someone holds on to an investment position they tend to be optimistic and bullish or at least hopeful that things will go up for them if they have been declining. But, as a bear market continues they feel more and more pain as it drops again and again to cause them to doubt. Eventually, the pain gets so bad that they sell. Some sell sooner than others, but bear markets come to an end when all who might sell do so.

What happens to people is that after they sell they become negative on the market. People's brains rationalize their decisions to make them feel like they have done the right thing. So if they get polled after they sold they'll declare themselves to be bears in the belief that the market will fall more after they sold.

The effect of all of this is that widespread bearish sentiment dominates a market after a bear market and often during a stage one basing market as well. The market action causes people to sell. Bull markets actually start after all who can sell do sell, so widespread bearish sentiment can actually be a positive for markets.

When a bull market starts almost no one believes it's a bull market, because they have seen so many rallies in the past twelve months and during the previous bear market fail. They don't want to get trapped in another one again so they just don't believe it's real. That's why few people are ever in at the start of a new bull market and the masses are incapable of investing in one. To do so requires going against the crowd and they cannot get themselves to do that.

There is a saying that a bull market climbs a wall of worry, and it's true. What this means is that it takes continued rallies and a long bull market for the worries of the masses to go away and for them to start to believe in the stock market again.

If you look at what happened after the 2008 stock market crash the statistics show that the individual investors in the United States actually sold more stocks than they bought in the first few years of the bull market that began in 2009. Many simply moved money out of stocks and into CD's that paid them practically nothing in fear of another 2008 crash.

It wasn't until the second half of 2013 that the masses started to get back into the US stock market in any meaningful way. By then, the stock market had already gone up for years and had reached a high valuation level. But they didn't care. All they knew was that stocks had now been going up for a long-time so they expected them to keep going higher and they didn't want to miss out anymore. The nightmare of 2008 had finally faded away from their brains and was replaced by a fear of missing out on more gains.

As a result, by January of 2014, over sixty-percent of respondents to the Investors Intelligence survey proclaimed themselves to be bullish on the stock market. This was a level seen the last two times in October of 2007, right at the last bull market top, and a few weeks before the 1987 stock market crash. After a first quick correction in October of 2014 played out the people bearish on the stock market all but disappeared. So in the first few months of 2015 the number of people declaring themselves to be bearish in the stock market in this survey fell to a level so low that it hadn't been seen in decades. In fact the last time it got so low was before the 1987 stock market crash.

As 2015 continued Ameritrade data showed even more signs of wild bullish sentiment among individual investors with its Ameritrade Index (IMX). This index, which is based upon the data of millions of Ameritrade brokerage accounts, showed that people went wild buying stocks to the point that many were in fact fully invested and even on margin. As the S&P 500 peaked out in May and the Nasdaq did in July, Ameritrade released a press release that said when it came to June, "TD Ameritrade clients were net buyers of equities for a second month in a row, which helped the IMX register its second largest month-to-month increase since tracking began in December 2012. Similar to the activity in May, increases in volatility for some of the most widely held names and relatively low volatility in the S&P 500 helped to boost the IMX reading." Even though the market was going sideways to nowhere people were more bullish than ever before. In July among the top stocks bought by people using Ameritrade accounts was Disney. It had been one of the top performing DOW stocks up to that point. In August it promptly collapsed after reporting disappointing earnings and sparked an across the board sell-off in the nation's leading media stocks, many of which fell over 10% in a single day.

High stock valuations also tend to come at a key top in a bull market and by 2012 the US stock market reached such a high valuation level that not even stock market bulls denied it. What they argued was that high valuations were justified on the basis that since interest rates were zero stocks were worth more. They also argued that valuations in themselves are not reliable indicators of what the stock market will do over the next twelve months, which is true. However, they are very important warning signs and are important when it comes to taking long-term investment decisions.

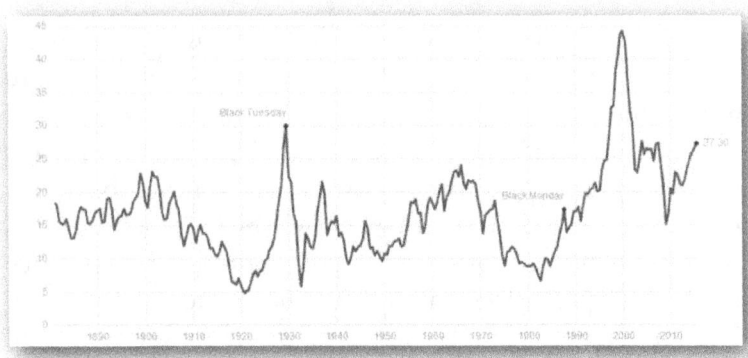

But more importantly, by 2015 we saw the US stock market as a whole reach such a crazed type of valuation level that it had been seen only three times in the entire history of the market. The cyclically adjusted P/E ratio (CAPE) for the S&P 500, which takes the average ten year P/E ratio and adjusts it for inflation, has only been higher two other times than it was in 2015: in 1929 and 2000.

The brutal truth is that the US stock market may never get this high ever again after the next bear market plays out for the rest of our lives in terms of valuations. When it peaked in 1929 it took almost 70 years for it to go to a bubble level again. Valuations do matter. Those that bought and invested at those peaks in the CAPE wiped themselves out. The best times to invest are when the CAPE gets below 10 like it last did in 1980. Extreme lows in valuation after giant bear markets bring secular bull markets that last for years.

For such lows in valuation one must look at Russia now or commodities and mining stocks as I will show you later in this book. Bear markets go on longer than anyone expects. How many gold bugs thought gold would fall for four years in 2011? It surprised me how long they fell and how low they got.

There is no reason to think that the US stock market cannot fall just like gold and silver did after they peaked in 2011. Now it does not have to fall 90% like it did after 1929 to get the CAPE under 10. In fact most of the times the CAPE got below ten was when inflation and high interest rates impacted the value of money to help distort the valuations of the stock market. That is what happened the last time the CAPE got below 10 in 1981. Remember the stagflation 1970's. And with us now facing an eventual bear market in bonds and coming commodity bull market something like that sort of process is likely to play out in the coming years. No matter though, we cannot predict everything perfectly. Smart investing is not about predicting, but about making changes when you see major turning moments in the market cycles play out. And that is exactly what I am trying to teach you in this book. In fact the implication of all of this is that we may actually be experiencing what will be a key turning point in our investment lifetimes.

The problem with looking at valuations and even sentiment is that they are not really great timing indicators. However, the third and final component that brings a major top for a stock market is. That consists of the fact that at a bull market top most stocks and sectors inside the stock market actually stop going up so that it is only a few stocks that drive the market higher. What happens is that everything gets so overvalued that sellers prevent it from going up and yet the market averages seem ok. What is happening is that a mania develops in a couple of stocks that attract manic buying at the very end of a bull market so that all of the bulls focus on those stocks and ignore everything else that is happening inside the stock market itself. Most people end up chasing these final winners and getting trapped in a massive top.

This process played out in the stock market this summer. Now the last time I saw this happen in a market in a dramatic way was actually back in 2011 with gold, silver, and mining stocks when they last made a bull market cycle top.

Look at the chart very carefully. In October of 2008 the HUI mining stock index, gold, and silver all bottomed and went up in a bull cycle that ended in the spring of 2011. In the above chart I have silver plotted out along with HUI mining stock index. They both went up together until 2011 and then suddenly silver began a parabolic move and doubled in price in roughly 90 days while the mining stocks simply sat there.

During the last month of that move though the mining stocks went sideways and gold barely went up too. In fact the mining stocks were off their highs of the year when silver made its final move up. In other words at the end of this bull market cycle in precious metals silver went straight up and people went crazy buying it at higher prices and chasing it, while nothing else in the precious metals complex went up anymore. This was the final buying panic at the end of that last bull market in the precious metals world.

At the same time silver was going up so fast that it made people get excited about it. It made them think that their mining stocks would go up huge too. But the stocks didn't. They didn't stop to ask themselves why?

The reason was simple though. Bull markets end in a buying panic like that in a small segment of the market. And when they end like that most things stop going up. And in this case silver was the one thing that kept going higher. That one big move in a few things makes everyone excited and they do not stop to think about what it means. Or they just do not know anything about market cycles to even realize that they should be concerned. But when that final buying panic ends the market tops and goes into a vicious bear market. So in July of 2015 silver was trading just under $15 and had fallen over 70% since its peak of 2011.

This same exact thing happened in October 2007 with the US stock market. At the final top of that US stock market bull market almost nothing went up anymore. But the market averages went up in October of 2007 in a final rally thanks to a few big moves in a few big cap tech stocks. Those moves caught everyone's attention and CNBC "Fast Money" boys banged the drum on them. Google, Amazon, and Apple all went up so much in the final weeks of that bull market that they alone helped create a final spurt in the Nasdaq. But almost nothing else went up with them in the final move. I pointed out to people that this was happening at the time and almost no one cared, because they were so caught up in the excitement on CNBC about these few stocks that they did not want to stop to think. And it is so hard for people to go against what they are being told by TV talking heads when they have been trained to obey them all of their lives.

To put it to you this way - when the stock market made its final top in October 2007 to mark the end of its stage three topping process a handful of big cap tech stocks played the same role that silver did in 2011 when the precious metals complex topped out. The same exact thing happened again in the US stock market in the summer of 2015 and suggests to me we saw a major top in the stock market form several months ago and are now at the start of a devastating bear market as we begin the month of September.

The S&P 500 last made a top in May of 2015. The market averages then fell to their long-term 150 and 200-day moving averages and bounced off of them in the beginning of July. That bounce led to a rally in the Nasdaq to a new 52-week high while the S&P 500 and DOW failed to make a new high and neither did the Russell 2000.

During that last move down though in May and June the internals of the stock market deteriorated rapidly, just like they did in August of 2007. Then when the Nasdaq made a new high in July they barely improved.

What happened is that most stocks did not go up at all during the final move up in the stock market. The final summer rally was driven by just a few stocks. The S&P 500 and Nasdaq 100 are weighted by market cap so the biggest market cap stocks help make it go up while the DOW is weighted by the price values of the stocks in it. The final move in the Nasdaq was really driven by a dozen of these big cap tech stocks while almost nothing else went up in a meaningful way.

To give you an example of what happened on Friday July 17, 2015, the Nasdaq went up 46.91 points. Google announced earnings on that day and went up so much that it was more responsible than 415 of the other stocks in the S&P 500 for the gains in that index on that day. Google went up 16% on earnings news so it helped create a 2 point gain in the S&P 500 when almost every other stock in it fell. Facebook also went up 4% so it helped the Nasdaq 100 even more with the combined efforts of Google. In fact 58% of the stocks in the Nasdaq finished the day down while 70% of the stocks in the NYSE closed the day in the red. And after the close CNBC "Fast Money" boys pumped Google and said buy tech stocks for more gains. Someone who watched this talk on CNBC would have thought that the entire stock market was on fire when it was actually dying. All traders saw was the final buying panic of the stage three top in a few final winners. On the next day, July 20, 2015, the Nasdaq made a final top.

Here is a chart of the percentage of stocks above their 200-day moving averages that trade on the NYSE. A stock or market begins a new bear market when it slips below its 200-day moving average and then that moving average acts as resistance as that is what creates a stage four bear market.

As you can see the internals of the US stock market topped out in 2014 and then diverged away from the stock market indices. But in May, they began a rapid deterioration and in June most stocks fell below their 200-day moving averages and then failed to rally back up above them despite the fact that the Nasdaq made a final high in July.

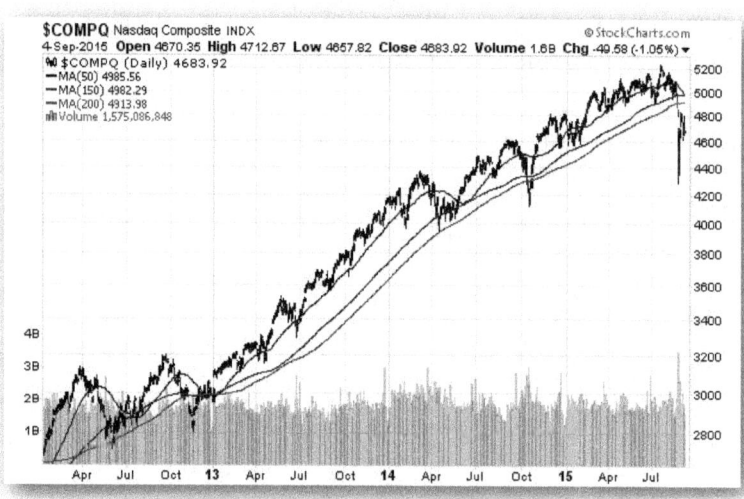

The internal structure of the market has completed a top in the stock market and rolled over, just as it did in the Fall of 2007. It means that the trend in the market is down.

A stage three top was completed in the summer of 2015 and as the final draft of this book is completed on September 8, 2015 the US stock market is now in a bear market. The question you need to ask yourself is what do you want to do about this?

CHAPTER 3
MANAGING RISK IN A BEAR MARKET

A lot of people define a bear market as a stock market that has fallen over twenty percent. The problem is that is not a very helpful definition, because it isn't very comforting to realize that you are in a bear market after you lose twenty percent of your money. The way I identify a bear market is when a market is in a stage four decline. When this happens the market averages are below their long-term 150 and 200-day moving averages and those moving averages are now acting as resistance. This is the situation the stock market is in as this book goes to publication.

I have been in two previous US stock market bear market cycles and have experience in knowing what people tend to do in them from communicating with thousands of investors over the years. Unfortunately what most people do is try to deny what is happening. The typical person with a brokerage account doesn't really spend a lot of time studying the market or thinking about what they are doing. They just buy and assume things will go up practically forever.

So when they get a brokerage statement in the mail with losses they just set it aside until the months go by and the losses pile up so much that they can no longer stand it. Then they sell out of the stock market and convince themselves that the losses were not their fault, but were caused by trading robots, stock market manipulators, or some other outside forces. Such people usually then get caught up trying to make money in some other financial bubble and repeating the same mistakes again. There are people who played tech stocks in 1999 and lost and then get caught up in the real estate mania a few years after that and lost again.

The other group of people are active traders. Unfortunately most of them tend to only think in one direction of the market and that is up. So in bear markets as a market declines they look for bottoms to play and when the market has rallies they buy into them expecting giant gains to come only to get caught up in bear market traps that crush them.

The problem is that a bear market is a market that trends down by making lower lows and lower highs. The way to make money from that is to ride that trend by using rallies to bet against stocks. This takes using a different trading strategy than the types of methods that work in a bull market. That means adapting and adjusting to a new market environment and it takes time for active traders to realize what is happening and then adjust. Some do it quickly, but most don't do it until the bear cycle is near its end.

In the end bear markets cause most people, whether they be amateur investors or professional traders, to lose money. Ironically though a bear market cycle actually provides us with the best opportunities to make money in the financial markets. You see they enable you to eventually buy into the stock market and individual stocks at super low prices once they run their course. They enable you to make money by betting against stocks and, because stocks tend to go down faster than they go up, the returns can come quickly when things drop. And finally they still enable you to invest in the few sectors and asset classes that breakaway from the overall bear trend and go into new bull markets. So yes there are wonderful opportunities to actually profit from the mess a bear market creates and I'll talk about all of these things in a bit.

First I need to talk about the topic of money management with you and some of the most important things that will determine your long-term success in the financial markets. Almost everything you ever hear from the financial media and even investing books is all about what you need to buy next. Television trading programs consist mainly of people yelling new stock picks at you with no regard to the overall trend of the market or the risks you may be taking. But times are different and I know you now may be asking yourself what should you do about the bear market?

The number one thing you need to is to decrease the risks you are taking in the financial markets. When bear markets hit the US stock market you must lower your exposure to the US stock market. Most people are trained to believe that if they just buy stocks and bonds that they will eventually get rich. But bear markets and this bear market in particular make that game plan very difficult to execute when put into action.

Over the past year I have said in interviews I have done on radio shows and internet podcasts that people need to raise up at least a ten percent cash position and put another ten percent of their money into gold. I have warned in these interviews that a bear market was coming and that no one can call the top of the bull market so everyone should do some selling and preparation ahead of time. The idea was that if they have some cash reserves they will lose less money and be able to buy at lower levels later and that the gold can provide some diversification for them and actually go up as the bear trend continues. It's a simple basic thing people can still do that can help and is something I can say in a few sentences for an interview, but I actually think people need to do more than that at this point. People really need to focus seriously on how they are managing their money and the risks they are taking. And now that we are really in a bear market it is time to take real action.

Bull markets provide people with an illusion that it is easy to make money in the stock market. It makes it look like all they have to do is buy stocks and have fun. And as a bull market goes up people get more and more excited and actually become lazy about what they are actually doing. They stop measuring the risks they are taking and end up in a total mess when the bear market begins. Nothing goes up nonstop forever.

Successful investing in the long-run takes work. And part of that work is avoiding the big mistakes people make and managing money in a way to limit the risks you are taking in order to maximize the gains you can make over time.

The single biggest mistake people make in the financial markets is to dedicate their entire financial lives to one market. Most bulls and bears do this. But real investing means spreading out in a mix of asset classes. Most US stock market bulls own nothing but investments linked to the US stock market and US bonds and think they are diversified when they are not.

At the same time often people who do not like the US stock market tend put all of their money on one bet, such as only investing in gold or by only trying to short the US stock market and make the same mistake.

Betting on one single market or one single trend may work for a period of time. It can work for years, but it always catches up with people in the end. Instead of putting their money to work with real investment principles they are more than happy to gamble their entire financial lives on the hopes that one market will go up forever or one trend will last forever. If you have suffered in the 2008 stock market crash you should never put yourself in a position to suffer like that again. All you need to do is diversify into a mix of asset classes and markets.

If you go into a Barnes and Noble you'll have a difficult time finding books about this topic, because they do not sell well, but there are some books that do discuss this in detail. I can recommend getting Mebane Faber's book titled The Ivy Portfolio. This book explains how the best performing and largest institutional endowments successfully spread their money out into an entire mix of investments classes so that they barely lose money in bear markets and beat almost all other money managers in the long run.

One of the best performing institutional investment operations in the world is the Yale Endowment fund run by

David Swenson. He has written several books for both lay readers and professionals about investing that are worth taking your time to read too. He only puts a small amount of the firm's money into the US stock market every year and still almost beats it every single year no matter what it does. Grab his books Unconventional Success and Pioneering Portfolio Management.

If you are going to be successful in the markets overtime you are going to have to be willing to always be learning. I know that everything gets presented to you in order to play on the idea of making the one giant killing. People like to believe all they need to do is buy a couple of stock picks and they can get rich. But even if they strike it big on a stock pick if they do not know how to manage their money they will end up losing their profits in time.

They essentially turn the stock market into their own private casino. Walk into any casino and you'll find that almost no one makes any money except the casino. But a few gamblers have made money and the way they have done so is not by predicting how each of their bets will turn out accurately every single time, but by applying money management techniques and mathematical concepts to put the odds in their favor. As a stock market player you can learn from that.

One of the best books about such people is Fortune's Formula by William Poundstone. One of the stories it recounts is about the man who invented counting cards when it comes to blackjack. This was a man named Edward Thorp who wrote a famous gambling book about it called Beat the Dealer. People focus on the counting cards aspect, but it really works because of the way the system manages the bets. It looks for times of a 5% advantage and then does something similar to the Kelly criterion betting system, which essentially bets by using a fixed percentage of a bankroll as it grows or shrinks.

The most successful casino betting systems are based on it. Thorp eventually couldn't go in casinos and count cards without getting banned so he had people go into sports book rooms for him and used the Kelly system to make millions on games where he thought he had a 5% edge on the odds. When the bags of money got too big he started to think it would be too dangerous for his agents to go into casinos with them. So for fun he went to the race track and did the same thing there. Then he started what was one of the most successful hedge fund partnerships of the 1970 and 1980's. Thorp wasn't the only mathematician to study gambling and stock investing. There were several key ones who wrote studies over the decades about money management and stock returns based on the Kelly criterion. Today they are the basis of what is called in academia quantitative finance.

They also provide the theoretical basis for trading and investing strategies today used by hedge funds and institutional investors. They are being used in computer trading and in portfolio asset allocation systems. This is really a new field that has emerged in the past twenty years. One of the key figures in the field was Claude Shannon, who graduated from MIT at the age of 21. He was one of the top cryptographers for the US military during World War II, but more importantly is known as the founder of computer "information theory" and came up with the basics of "circuit design" in 1937. He created Boolean theory which is the basis of computer language.

For fun he hung out with Edward Thorp and also got interested, perhaps obsessed, with the stock market. Between 1966 and 1971 he gave a series of talks to a packed lecture hall at MIT about the stock market. At one of them he revealed a mathematical discovery. His friend's called it "Shannon's demon."

He said that you could make money off of the movements of stocks without knowing what direction they were going to move. Imagine a volatile stock that simply moves randomly up and down every single day. Put half of your money into that stock and half into cash in your brokerage account.

At noon every day you rebalance your portfolio to maintain this 50/50 asset allocation. So if by noon the stock goes up you sell some of the stock to realize the profits and move them into cash to maintain the 50/50 balance. If instead at noon the stock were to be down you would buy extra shares with the cash to get back to the 50/50 allocation.

Now imagine that the stock doubles one day and then falls in half the next. And then day after day makes similar giant moves up and down. And you rebalance your account every single day to maintain the 50/50 asset allocation. In a short period of time you would amass a fortune. Not only that, but the results would actually be LESS volatile than if one simply put 100% of their money into the stock and held it. In fact in that case odds are they would make hardly anything.

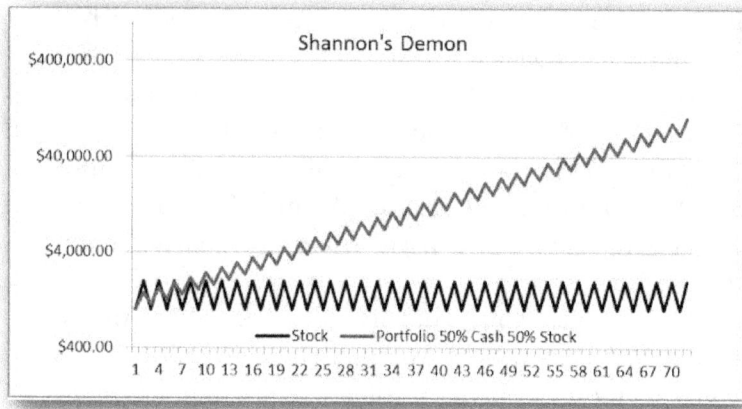

What happens is when the stock goes up you sell some of it and when it goes down you buy some of it in order to maintain the 50/50 asset balance. Simulations show that if you started out doing this with $1.00 on a stock that doubles or falls in half every single day in 240 days that one single dollar would turn into a million.

How does this happen? It's mathematical magic. The arithmetic mean return is higher than the geometric mean. All of the up days add up if the profits are partially realized. What is being harvested is volatility.

Now after Shannon gave this presentation someone asked him the obvious question, which is why doesn't he do this himself? The answer is simple. The commissions would eat you alive and you would need a stock so volatile that it either doubles or falls in half every single day.

Other mathematicians have built off of this idea though. One is Thomas Cover who did a study to see what would happen if you owned every single stock in the stock market and rebalanced a portfolio so it owned the same fixed percentage of them every single day. Guess what happened. It beat the market.

Of course you may wonder who wants to do that with every stock in the stock market, because the transaction costs would be extreme. Well, some of the largest hedge funds and institutional investors in the world are rebalancing their portfolios like this every single day. I believe it is their secret to success.

I have mentioned the book the Ivy Portfolio by Mebane Faber earlier. It examines the Yale and Harvard endowment funds that have beat the stock market over the past decade by investing in a diverse mix of asset classes. These two funds maintain a fixed rate of asset allocation every single year. They never have more than 15% of their money for example invested in the US stock market and yet they still beat the market.

The book is worth buying to understand asset allocation. But one thing that is really helping them beat the market is that they are rebalancing their portfolio every single day. These funds are beating the market with billions of dollars under management and barely lost anything during the 2008 stock market crash. They are applying the concept of volatility harvesting strategy that Claude Shannon revealed in his speech to boost returns their and lower the volatility of their entire portfolio as a whole.

The ideal portfolio that is as close to perfect as you can get from a risk to reward standpoint is one that is invested in a mix of markets and assets that are as uncorrelated with one another as possible and has no more than twenty-percent of its money devoted to any one single asset class or market. By uncorrelated what I mean is that the markets and asset classes being invested in are not trading together. So when one goes up another goes down or they really have no relationship to one another at all. Such a portfolio would hardly ever lose any money to amount to anything and is likely to beat the US stock market every single year, unless there is a fluke year off of a bear market bottom in which it is up 100% or something.

Of course there is no perfect mix of five assets that are totally uncorrelated with another and the correlation relationship between two different assets can change from time to time. But we have to think in such an ideal to think and work towards it. And it is this that the Yale and Harvard money managers are really providing to their investors even if the uninitiated imagines that it is super stock picking research and predictions about the future that they are good at. If you are curious you can examine the correlation between various ETF's and stocks of your choice by going to the website investpy.com. It has a tool you can use to do this.

I have used an institutional portfolio management computer program to run simulations using historical data to study rebalancing strategies. One thing I have found is that if you use ETF's you do not need to do daily rebalancing, because there is not much difference in the end result between daily and weekly rebalancing. Monthly rebalancing is better than none at all, but weekly seems to be best. Annual would be better than nothing, but isn't that much better than doing nothing to get better gains. It's good though for preventing losses.

Let me show you some simple interesting examples. Think about the US stock market. It has gone up a lot since 2009 and US stock market bulls at the moment are extremely bulled up. If you talk to them they will tell you that the only thing worth investing in is the US stock market and if you had put all of your money in just the S&P 500 ETF a few years ago then you would have made a fortune so you should do that right now. Of course you would have suffered in 2008, but that is a distant memory right now.

If you would have put all of your money into the SPY ETF that tracks the S&P 500 on January 1, 2007 you would be up about 55% from that date till the end of 2014. You also would have suffered through a 67% decline during the 2007-2009 bear market.

Now something interesting would have happened if you would have put half of your money into TLT, which is the ETF for the year 20-year US Treasury bond, and half into SPY starting on January 1, 2007. Now from then till the end of 2014 TLT went up 34% so it is up much less than the gain realized by SPY since then. So if you would have put half your money in both starting then and just watched it all you would have been up 44.50% by the end of 2014. Now you would have had a smaller drawdown during the 2008-2009 bear market so you would have been very happy then, but today you might be regretful about now having made 55%. But in turn someone can say that the safety of being more diversified now and not losing your ass in 2008 was worth making a little less.

However, if you put half your money in both the TLT and SPY and rebalanced those positions every week to maintain the 50/50 ratio something interesting would have happened. You would have made a 63% return by now and only been down roughly 22% during the nasty bear market of 2007-2009 instead of the 67% drawdown suffered by those invested only in the S&P 500 during that time. In other words a portfolio that was 50/50 invested in US stocks and bonds and rebalanced to maintain that 50/50 ratio every single week would have generated market returns that beat not only the US stock market, but just about every single hedge fund and money manager on the planet. And it would have done that with less risk.

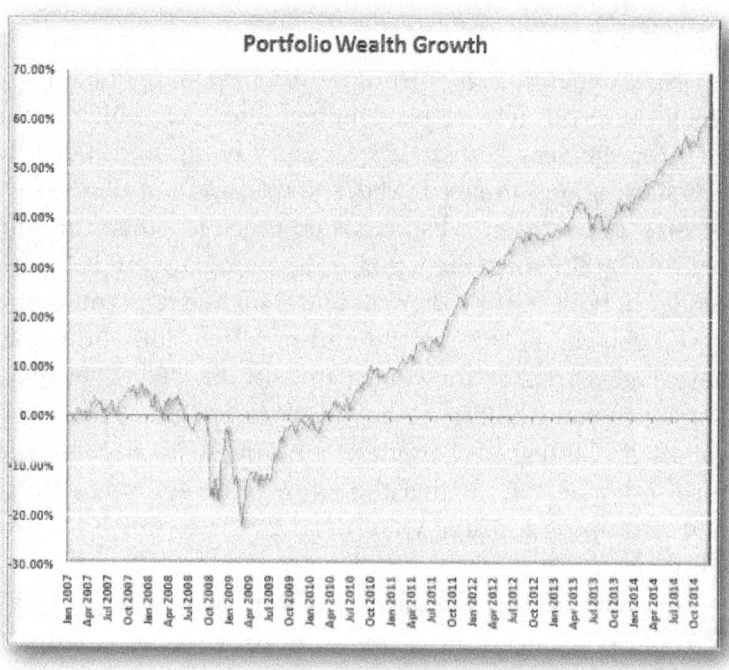

This is the magic of volatility harvesting and portfolio rebalancing. It can generate bigger returns with less risk if the portfolio is invested in the right mix of asset classes. The reason why TLT would have helped supercharge a portfolio mixed with SPY is because those two assets have had a negative correlation with one another during this time frame.

You have been trained to think that the way to make the most money in the stock market is to be fully invested in it. People are so scared to reduce their stock market positions out of fear of missing out on big gains. This is why so many cannot sell even when they know a bear market is coming. But if they realized that diversification and rebalancing can actually make them more money and reduce their risk at the same time then they would not be fooled into thinking that they should not reduce their US stock market exposure.

I have seen many Wall Street experts claim that you should not own gold, because if you own gold you may miss out on having that money in the stock market. But what would have happened if you would have added gold, through the GLD ETF to this back test? From January 1, 2007 till the end of 2014 gold prices went up 37%, which is in line with what TLT has done, but is behind the 55% gain generated by S&P 500. This seems to back up the argument that if you owned gold you would have missed out. But this is wrong. You see if 33% of your money had been placed into a portfolio evenly in GLD, SPY, and TLT on January 1, 2007 the results by the end of 2014 would have been incredible. Such a portfolio would have gone up over 70% and would have only been down 3.27% at its worst drawdown point during the 2007-2009 bear market.

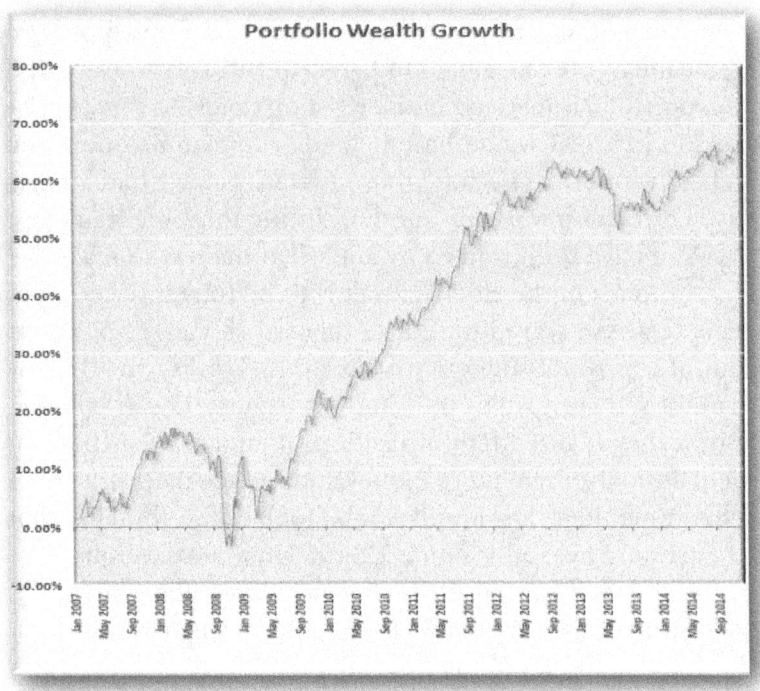

Gold, TLT, and SPY have all been negatively correlated with one another since 2007. There are a lot of implications to all of this. One obvious one is that gold can play an important role in any portfolio. In fact I would argue that you actually now need gold in your portfolio if you do not have any in it. I'll talk more about gold later with you.

However, I am not suggesting that you put 1/3 of your money in GLD, TLT, and SPY as in the this last example, although such a mix that is rebalanced every week is likely to continue to do better than simply owning the US stock market for the next few years. What I am suggesting though that for one to have 100% of their money only invested in the US stock market right now is total foolishness. Not only do you risk a large loss if I am right about this bear market, but it's not necessary to be 100% invested in the US stock market either in order to beat it. In fact it's just a damn dumb thing to do. If you are 100% invested in the US stock market for goodness sake DIVERSIFY!!!!! Do not become a DOW DUMMY no matter what the TV tells you to do!

I am convinced that this rebalancing magic is the key thing driving the investment returns of some of the largest institutional investors today operating inside the stock market. If you look at their annual reports few of them though own gold right now. One thing that is making rebalancing work for them is the big position almost all of them have in bonds, because of the fact that they have tended to go up when the US stock market falls.

I do not think this is going to happen this year, but at some point in the future, and it may be a few years away from today, I fear a time will come in which US bonds will go into a bear market while the stock market is falling too.

If Treasury bonds were to go into a bear market as the stock market is declining than all of these giant institutional players will have to find a rebalancing replacement for them. They will be FORCED to do so. And that means that they will literally be FORCED to put money into gold. Gold prices would skyrockets as a result. Keep this point in your mind. Never forget it.

There are a lot of applications to using this type of math and analysis to investing. One level of investing is figuring out what is likely to go up and what stocks are good and then another level is applying this type of money management rebalancing to that analysis. One can keep things very simple though with ETF's and do powerful things to control the risk in one's account and work towards high returns at the same time. This stock market game is a competition in which the superior money managers and investors win. That's why I want to share with you the importance of money management earlier in this book instead of later on.

In the Power Investor group I put together a model portfolio that applies these concepts by rebalancing the positions in it every single Friday using the closing prices. This portfolio is invested in a basket of ETF's so it's an easy way for anyone to use these concepts in the real world as an investor.

CHAPTER 4

HOW TO BUY DURING A BEAR MARKET

There are ways to make money betting against stocks during a bear market and there are ways to actually make money going long in a bear market even though most people actually lose money. I bet against stocks in bear markets by using exchange traded funds that are designed to go up when the stock market drops, by purchasing puts on individual stocks, and by short selling individual stocks. I talk about all of these things in the Power Investor updates. Stocks tend to go down faster than they go up so when you hit things right the profits can come quickly. And having a portion of your portfolio dedicated to actually making money when the stock market declines is a great way to reduce the risk in your overall portfolio to market drops.

What does not work though is chasing the stocks that were the big winners in the last few years of a bull market even though that is exactly what most people try to do during a bear market. The funny thing about bear markets is that they actually bring with them some of the best opportunities to make money going long in the right things, and it isn't that hard to take advantage of them if you know how. I use these techniques to find investment ideas for the Power Investor groups and decide what exchange traded funds I want to own.

The problem is few people know how to do this. And I want to talk to you about how to buy in bear markets in a way that works. First though I want to tell you what does not work. There are two things most people do in a bear market. The first, which is what the average investor does, is to just try to ignore the losses and hope things go back up. Sometimes they just try to stop looking at their statements when they get them in the mail. Or they will just watch CNBC to hear people tell them that things are ok and believe them.

But the active trader does something different. What he tends to do is take on more risks by either doubling down on his trades or suddenly doing more frequent and manic trading. The trading methods that worked in the bull market stop working. Breakouts fail. Stocks drop when they "should" go up. But instead of adapting the typical active trader just goes nuts and compounds his losses.

In 1999 internet stocks were the rage and I was trading them by buying them when they would make a new 52-week high after a period of consolidation. It wasn't unusual for stocks to breakout like this and go up 30% in a few days! Sometimes they would even double. But then in March of 2000 these breakouts suddenly stopped working. Instead of going up they would breakout and go up for a few minutes and just come back down even though the stock market continued higher for a few weeks.

It was all a sign that the market had changed and a stage three top was being made. And so the stock market rolled over into a bear market that lasted for years. During that bear market every day Ameritrade would post on their website the most widely bought and sold stocks by their customers. This was what hundreds of thousands of people were doing. I'd watch it out of curiosity and I saw a very simple pattern.

What stocks people were buying were the ones that tended to go up the most in a single day. Such stocks attracted the manic traders. These could be stocks that had some news story or a big short squeeze day. But these stocks would not continue higher for long and within a few days would just fall back down and then they would get on the list of the most sold stocks on Ameritrade.

It was clear that the Ameritraders on a whole were destroying themselves. They were chasing fake rallies during a bear market in crazy stocks. They were engaging in manic trading and I'm sure most of them were simply addicted to what amounted to gambling action.

That is what most active traders do in a bear market. They do not short stocks. They do not adapt to the new trends of the market. They may have been making money during the bull market before, but those trades that worked before no longer work. They sit their confused, stressed, and essentially drain away their money.

But there are ways to make money by buying in a bear market. You just have to buy the right things and there are very few things that are going to go up for real. Yes, most things are just going to have temporary pops and then drop.

But the few things that go up for real can go up for years. What happens is that as the US stock market begins a new bear market a few sectors and even entire asset classes begin new bull markets. Those are the things to buy and hold or trade if you want to do short-term breakout trading. But they do not make the news and most active traders just obsess over the stocks that were once hot in the past.

What I want to talk about is how to identify the bullish turning points in these sectors and asset classes. In the first quarter of 2000 it was tobacco, utility stocks, and REIT's that began a new bull market as the US stock market rolled over into a new bear market. Take a look at the chart of Philip Morris (now Altria) above.

In the chart above MO is rising in price while the Nasdaq is shown falling in price during this time period. On the bottom is the relative strength plot of MO and the S&P 500. This line divides the price of MO with the price of the S&P 500 so it goes down when the price of MO performs worse than the S&P 500 and up when it performs better.

MO had been in a bear market for years and you can see how it fell into March of 2000. But it made a bottom in February and went into a very short stage one basing period. And it did this just as the US stock market rolled over into a bear market during a stage three base.

You can see how the relative strength line went sideways during this period and clearly turned up in April and rose for the rest of the year. The price of MO also went up for years as the US bear market continued until 2003.

The only things to buy during a bear market in the US stock market are sectors and asset classes that hold up while US market averages continue lower. When something has been in a bear market for years and then suddenly starts to hold up while the US stock market goes into a bear market it is showing you that something is changing for it.

Now the problem is that during a stage one base it can be very difficult to predict when that basing phase is going to end. That means that there are two ways to buy. The first way is to simply notice what is happening during the stage one base and take a small position. The position has to be small enough that you can take a 10% drop if it were to occur and be able to ride it out.

If you buy and hold a position like this then you will own a position when the market turns up and a new bull market starts. This is why even as I believed the stock market was beginning a near bear market and began to bet against the market in July of 2015 I still continued to hold some long positions in my own investment accounts and in the Power Investor model rebalancing portfolio.

The second way to know what to buy is to wait for the first move up through resistance and the stage one base. You see the breakout and you see that the sector or asset class is performing better than the US stock market when the market drops. Then you wait for a consolidation period to buy into.

So with MO for example if you would have looked at it in June of 2000 you would have seen what happened and realized that a new bull market had begun. You could then let it go sideways and try to buy a dip or bought it when it broke through the $3.50 level that September.

And take a look at this stock chart of Duke Energy. You can see that it made a double bottom in March of 2000 at the same time that the Nasdaq rolled over. It started a bull market at that moment. Notice how the relative strength line for it went sideways in the first few months of 2000 and then turned up to show that it was outperforming the US stock market averages as they went into decline.

Despite the great action in these stocks neither one of these two stocks became one of the most bought stocks on Ameritrade during these months, because the Ameritraders kept trying to buy and trade the stocks that were hot the year before. They could not stop themselves, even though there were actually incredible ways to make money going long. There were just only a few sectors going up though and they did not know what they were and their TV's would not tell them.

RWT was a REIT I remember back then too. It did the same thing as MO and DUK by completing a stage one base in the first quarter of 2000 and then starting a new bull market. Now RWT did not go up at the exact same moment that DUK or MO did. In fact none of these stocks traded exactly in synch with each other. They completed their stage one bases at different times than the others did.

Now other sectors and even entire stock markets also began new bull markets later during the US stock market bear market of 2000. The Russian stock market for example had a crash in 1998. But in 2001 it began to outperform the US stock market as it went through a stage one basing phase.

As the US stock market made lower lows in 2001 Russia held up, as you can see from the Templeton Russia Fund. After 9/11 the TRF fund completed its stage one base and began a bull market that lasted for years while the US stock market continued lower once again into the summer of 2002.

Look at this chart above, because it is the single best way to make money invested in any market. The best opportunities to make money are actually during US stock market bear markets. You find them by looking for sectors, asset classes, and stock markets outside of the US that hold up while the US stock market goes down. Then you invest in them.

When they hold up during US stock market bear attacks they show you that they are getting ready to go up and that most of the risks are gone. They also tend to do this after they have already gone through big bear market cycles of their own and are at truly cheap valuation levels.

Now none of this is a recommendation to buy DUK, MO, RWT, or even Russia at this moment. Russia is something I will likely invest in sometime in the future, but tobacco stocks, utility stocks, and REIT's are not good investments today, because they are not in the position they were in 2000. Instead they are actually trading worse than the US stock market is right now! You see very bear cycle in the US stock market is a little different than the ones that have come before it.

In 2007 it was bonds and the TLT ETF that began a new bull market as the US stock market rolled over and completed a stage three top during the months of July through October. During those months the internals of the US stock market went into collapse. They turned down in July just as they did during the summer months of 2015. During those months though stock market bubble bulls ignored all of that and said that the Fed was going to lower interest rates so there was nothing to worry about.

Of course the market began a bear market collapse in the fourth quarter of 2007 and then totally crashed in the fall of 2008. But in August of 2007 when the TLT ETF went through the $67.50 level it completed a stage one base and went into a new bull market. Anyone who owned it or bought it then make huge gains from that position while everyone else watched their wealth drip away during the repeated US stock market bear attacks that followed.

So what is in a position to go into a new bull market and breakaway from the US bear market trend now? Well TLT appears to be in a giant topping formation and yet is outperforming the US stock market at the moment. So it looks to me like it will be decent going into the end of this year, but is not in a great investment buy position to provide great gains like it did in the last bear market.

Instead you need to look for asset classes, sectors, and markets that were in the same position that tobacco, utility stocks, and REIT's were in back in 2000. That means you need to look for areas of the global markets that began bear markets a long time ago, got cheap, and are in a position to begin new bull markets at some point in the coming months ahead of a stock market bear market bottom. These are the type of opportunities that have the best chance to become breakaway bull markets even if they have not done so yet.

The main things to watch for now are Russia and commodities. In my opinion a portion of money in typical US stock market funds and investments should be rotated into these areas and into cash reserves or active bets against the US stock market.

Gold and silver for example both last made bull markets tops way back in 2011. Both have been in a stage one base for almost two years. Both have relative strength plots that are now flattening out after they have been in an extended decline for three years.

What that means is that they lagged the US stock market for years, but are no longer lagging the US stock market. That tells us that they are in a position to breakout and begin new bull markets. For gold to do that it will have to now go above the $1,175 area of it's last high. This is also where it's 200-day moving average currently is resting at. Silver's resistance price is now $16.00. The problem is I have no way of predicting what day or what week such a breakout will occur. So this is a situation I'm monitoring very closely.

What about oil? Well oil stocks are not in a good position right now, because they started a bear market last year. They are still lagging the US stock market. I do think that maybe in a year they will start to hold up against the US stock market and begin a new bull market. Gold for example did not start to hold up against the US stock market in the 2000-2003 bear market until 2001 and then it began a full blown bull market in 20002. So oil could be a good game in the future. There will be things to buy and things to invest in and this relationship of performance against the US stock market during bear declines will be the key thing to keep your eye on in order to identify the best investments to make on the long side of the markets in the years ahead. I will certainly be doing this in updates for the Power Investor group.

CHAPTER 5

THE DEBT DANGER AND GOLD

Those that invest in gold may in fact become the biggest winners of this bear market in the stock market. As I write this gold is still locked in a stage one base, but is displaying signs that it is outperforming the United States stock market. That means that it is likely to breakout into a new bull market at some point in the coming months. A lot of people say that gold is going to go up, because they believe that the United States government is going to go bankrupt one day. In reality, it already did years ago. I can tell you the exact moment it happened. The date this happened was on August, 15, 1971. Understanding this is the key to discovering what is ultimately going to drive this bear market in the stock market. What happened on that day?

Well, a lot of events led to that moment. In order to tell you the story behind that day you must understand that the United States became the most powerful nation in the world after World War II. The rest of the world got bombed out by that war and had to rebuild. Japan was devastated and so were Europe and Russia. But the US was not hurt. It came out of the war in a position of economic and military dominance.

In terms of military power, the United States dropped two atomic bombs on Japan. These were the most powerful weapon detonations ever used in the history of warfare and the US was the only nation in the world with such weapons at that time. As a result, the United States now had the most powerful military ever seen in human history.

The United States also came out of the war in a position of great economic power. With its factories still intact, it became a great exporter to the rest of the world. It was also a lender of money to the rest of the world. In the years following the war, it created global economic institutions such as the International Monetary Fund and the World Bank. It helped create the United Nations, and it is no coincidence that the UN headquarters was built in New York City.

After World War II, the United States evolved from being a continental republic into being a global empire. In the next few decades, the nation became something much different from what the founding fathers created. Before World War II, the United States never had a large permanent standing army and hardly anyone paid any income taxes. The government didn't need much tax revenue, because it was small in size.

But in the years following World War II, the United States became involved in the Cold War. So it kept its new big army and turned the "War Department" into the "Department of Defense." It created a Central Intelligence Agency to covertly intervene in smaller nations throughout the world and keep them on the right side. Black ops, black bag money campaigns, and even assassination programs became a part of what CIA people called "the great game."

The United States became involved in an expensive nuclear arms race against the Soviet Union. Defense spending exploded and a new military-industrial complex rose in the United States. A new "power elite" emerged behind the scenes that came to make most of the big decisions when it came to war and peace and foreign affairs. The United States government had a "national security state" within it that grew in immense power. The federal government became a big government warfare/welfare state with giant expenditures that required big taxes and eventually big debts.

I tell the story of how this all happened from 1945 until 1963 in my book The War State. If you have not read it yet then you should read it after you read this book. Today you'll find that when you factor in the interest on the national debt from past wars plus total defense expenditures that United States spends almost 40% of its federal budget on the military. It accounts for over 46% of total world arms spending.

The American defense department employees more people on the planet than any other enterprise on earth with 3.2 million American employees. To give you an idea of how big this is, the second largest employer inside the United States is Wal-Mart with 2.1 million employees and after that is McDonald's with 1.9 million people working for it. So a good portion of the American economy is dependent on the defense industry and the big government jobs tied to it, which creates a big burden on the private sector of the economy. These defense contractors receive no bid guaranteed cost plus contracts from the government and therefore do not act inside the free market price forces created by supply and demand, but feed off the productivity of others.

As he left office President Eisenhower gave a famous farewell address in which he said, "We must guard against the acquisition of unwarranted influence, whether sought or unsought, by the military-industrial complex. The potential for the disastrous rise of misplaced power exists and will persist." Today these words seem timeless.

What people really remember Ike saying is, "We must never let the weight of this combination endanger our liberties or democratic processes. We should take nothing for granted. Only an alert and knowledgeable citizenry can compel the proper meshing of the huge industrial and military machinery of defense with our peaceful methods and goals, so that security and liberty may prosper together."

What most people take away from this speech is a warning that the military-industrial complex could "endanger our liberties or democratic processes." However, in other speeches and in released records of private White House meetings, President Eisenhower expressed worries over the size of defense spending as being the real grave danger that would lead to great harm to liberties and democracy in the United States.

President Eisenhower worried that if the government spent more than it took in that it could end up running a big enough budget deficit to send the country "straight toward inflation of an uncontrollable character." That would mean the government would have to interfere in the private market to try to control inflation and keep defense spending going at the same time. The whole nation could become a warped "garrison state" as a result.

Eisenhower thought that anyone who didn't see this as a danger and understand "that national security and national solvency are mutually dependent, and that permanent maintenance of a crushing weight of military power would eventually create dictatorship, should not be entrusted with any kind of responsibility in our country." In one of his final cabinet meetings he asked, "Can free government overcome the many demands made by special interests and the indulgence of selfish motives?" Would the interests of the war state come to dominate the economy and warp American institutions and government?

Today, we are used to seeing giant budget deficits and people telling us not to worry about them. Vice-President Dick Cheney famously made the statement that "deficits don't matter" to Treasury Secretary Paul O'Neill who kept bugging him about them. But in the 1940's, 1950's and 1960's, Presidents Roosevelt, Truman, Eisenhower, and Kennedy all kept their eye on the budget and fought against the creation of big government spending deficits. They had to.

After World War the United States II created a monetary system that made the US dollar the reserve currency of the world that also put a lid on the growth of government spending deficits. It was called the Bretton Woods system and it made the United States the economic center of the world for decades by linking the US dollar to gold in the international currency markets.

The British Empire had linked the pound to gold during its time of world dominance and other nations followed its lead. But the debts of World War I and the Great Depression ended the world gold standard. In the closing months of

World War II, leaders from across the world met in Bretton Woods, New Hampshire to hammer out a new global monetary system.

Each nation agreed to tie the value of their currencies to the US dollar. To bolster faith in the dollar, the US agreed separately to link the dollar to gold at the rate of $35 per ounce of gold. At this price foreign governments and central banks were able to exchange dollars for gold.

Bretton Woods established a system of payments based on the dollar, in which all currencies were defined in relation to the dollar, itself convertible into gold, and above all, "as good as gold." The US currency was now effectively the world currency, the standard to which every other currency was pegged. As the world's key currency, most international transactions were denominated in US dollars.

The effect of this was that the US dollar was the currency with the most purchasing power and it was the only currency that was backed by gold. Additionally, all European nations that had been involved in World War II were highly in debt and transferred large amounts of gold into the United States, a fact that contributed to its world supremacy. Thus, the US dollar strongly appreciated in the rest of the world and, therefore, became the key currency of the Bretton Woods system.

The strong value of the US dollar helped the United States import goods at a cheaper price than other nations were able to do. It also made it easier to sell government debt in the form of Treasury bonds on the world market. After World War II, the United States actually ran giant trade surpluses as it exported manufacturing goods to the rest of the world. This helped to create a shortage of dollars in the world. One result was that the Truman administration launched the "Marshall Plan" to send aid to Europe to help it rebuild.

Bretton Woods and the end of World War II helped created a post-war boom in the American economy. A housing boom took off across the nation and so did a new boom in car manufacturing. President Eisenhower built a national highway system and a new consumer culture was born. The middle class grew and people felt very confident about the future.

But in time, a problem emerged. The Bretton Woods system put a limit on how much debt a nation could accumulate, because it demanded that dollars could be exchanged for gold in the international currency markets. To tell you how this worked, before Bretton Woods, the gold standard was used to back currencies. So the international value of currency was determined by its fixed relationship to gold and gold was used to settle international accounts. The gold standard maintained fixed exchange rates that were seen as desirable because they reduced the risk when trading with other countries.

Imbalances in international trade were theoretically rectified automatically by the gold standard. A country with a growing trade deficit and growing debts would have depleted gold reserves and would thus have to reduce its money supply. The resulting fall in demand would reduce imports and the lowering of prices would boost exports; thus the deficit would be rectified. Any country experiencing inflation would lose gold and, therefore, would have a decrease in the amount of money available to spend.

Eventually, this decrease in the amount of money would act to reduce the inflationary pressure. In effect, what the gold standard did was keep monetary order by limiting the amount of disorder government spending deficits and trade deficits could create. It acted as a brake on debt accumulation and government spending.

In theory, the new Bretton Woods system could do the same thing. And it did for a period of time. And it was during this time that the United States became great. But then, several things began to happen that caused people in Europe and Asia to slowly begin to transfer their dollars into gold. The United States began to generate small, but meaningful, trade and budget deficits.

Europe and Japan also began to rebuild themselves. Right after World War II, the US manufactured half of the world's goods. However, as they rebuilt their factories they began to export to the United States. But Presidents Eisenhower and Kennedy were able to make some small adjustments here and there that stopped the gold outflow.

The Johnson Presidency, though, ruined the nation's fiscal position. President Lyndon Johnson created big government spending deficits when he launched the Vietnam War and his social spending "war on poverty" programs he called the Great Society. He vastly increased government expenditures and did not raise taxes. The result was a deterioration in the position of the US trade deficit and an outflow of gold. The US economy grew, but inflation picked up and imbalances built up. Lyndon Johnson's response, and that of his successor President Nixon, was to pressure the US Federal Reserve into simply printing more money.

Both Presidents refused to make tough decisions. They did not demand that the American people tighten their belts and pay up for the Vietnam War and their social spending programs so foreign creditors simply demanded more of the nation's gold. What started as a trickle of gold flowing out of the nation became a tidal wave.

If all of the gold left the nation, than the US dollar would become worthless. The nation, in effect, was heading to bankruptcy, because it could not stop the gold outflow without raising taxes, reducing spending, and running a budget surplus. No Republican or Democrat wanted to do that so Nixon made a decision with a few of his closest advisors in secret. He did not even tell anyone in the US State Department. He decided to announce unilaterally to the world that the United States would no longer allow people to convert dollars into gold. He would shut the gold window.

He would make the US dollar a pure paper currency backed by nothing. The thing is, he wasn't sure what would happen. He was desperate. One of the men who helped create this plan for President Nixon even told him that they did not know what would happen after Nixon announced it, but he had to do it anyway. Nixon made the announcement on TV on August 15, 1971 by stating that the government would abandon the Bretton Woods agreements and no longer link the US dollar to the price of gold.

What came as a result was nine years of monetary chaos. Gold had been fixed to the dollar at $35 an ounce. Gold prices soared until they briefly went to $850 an ounce in 1980. During this time, inflation in the United States exploded and the economy went into a recession. Two years after Bretton

Woods the annual inflation rate hit 8%. By 1980, it was at 14%. At the same time, the stock market went nowhere so stock investors lost their ass thanks to inflation. OPEC put on an oil embargo that helped to drive gas prices up too. People who lived through this time remember this as the miserable Carter years of stagflation.

Toward the end of Jimmy Carter's presidency it became clear that someone had to do something to stop the inflation. Federal Reserve Chairman, Paul Volker, took action and jammed up interest rates to 20%. This, of course, caused a big recession in the first year of Ronald Reagan's Presidency. Housing markets got smashed and many people in debt went bankrupt. Small farmers got wiped out.

But eventually, the situation stabilized. The high interest rates caused gold prices to fall and inflation fell close to zero. Other nations followed the lead of the United States and simply floated their currencies on the world market too. Now currencies fluctuated in value. Now the United States no longer needed gold to finance its deficits. It could simply print money out of thin air.

However, the United States was still the biggest economy in the world with the biggest military machine ever seen in human history. So, without any other nation going back to a gold standard, the US dollar still maintained its dominance. Paul Volker's actions brought confidence, and once he finished defeating inflation and began to lower rates, a new economic boom took place in the United States. President Ronald Reagan cut taxes and people were happy.

But, as the years went by, two things happened underneath the surface prosperity. Pure fiat currency leads to sickness. First, financial speculation came to dominate the economy. A monetary system based on money printing created wild gyrations in financial markets all over the world that speculators were able to take advantage of. A giant secular stock market boom was one result. If you look at a chart of the United States stock market since its inception and you'll see that its rate of advance accelerated in the 1980's. It went on a slow upward slope in the 1800's with lots of ups and downs and continued higher on a slow trajectory until 1980. Then it began to go up at a parabolic rate. The reason was not because the U.S. economy was suddenly growing faster than it ever had before in history, but because the collapse of Bretton Woods and a pure paper currency helped contribute to money printing and speculation that helped create an accelerating stock market boom.

A bull market culture in equities grew. A decade of captivating gains brought the masses into the stock market in the 1990's. They believed in the market. Big debts led to big trade imbalances. Manufacturing in the United States shrank, but the finance sector grew. By 2003, 40% of corporate profits were generated in the finance industry.

Debt troubles came though. Paper currency debts enabled nations and companies to use debt to grow and profit. One debt crises after another erupted periodically in third world nations as hot speculative finance went in and out of places such as Mexico and Argentina. Even South Korea suffered from one.

A debt crisis also hit the Savings and Loan industry in the United States around 1990. Financial volatility grew. One result was the 1987 stock market crash. Another was the internet bubble of the 1990's and the 2000 stock market bust. Another was a real estate bubble that grew in the last decade and the stock market crash of 2008.

The crash of 2008 brought heavily indebted Wall Street banks to the edge of bankruptcy. To stop that the Federal Reserve and Treasury Department created a bailout program, giving banks over a trillion dollars. As a result, the United States budget deficit exploded to a trillion dollars in 2008 and the Federal Reserve took toxic junk debts off the books of bankers and put them on its own balance sheets.

Wall Street won and the stock market went back up, but the US economy has been in a horrible recession ever since. The middle class lost a lot of its wealth and as a whole has shrunk. Dependency on government programs such as food stamps and unemployment benefits on the part of the masses is now just a regular part of everyday life for millions of Americans. The United States has become more of a two-class society, but corporate profits for financial companies and companies well connected to the government have exploded over the past few years.

This is a lot of history you probably already knew, but when you sit back and put everything in context you see there are two key things to take away from it. First, the end of Bretton Woods on August 15, 1971, was a turning point in the history of the United States and the American economy. It was the only way to keep the out of control big government warfare/welfare system going.

Deficit spending became the only way to fund the Reagan defense boom and the war on terror and the welfare programs without putting big taxes on people. It was the only way to keep piling up big debts. And people came to not only like the system, but many came to love it, because they benefited from rising housing prices and rising stock market prices. The so called one-percent got richer and many in the middle class saw the equity bull market as a way to get rich too. So, when the crash of 2008 came few asked any questions. And few have protested ever since. Few worry about the growth of government and such things as NSA spy programs, because so many benefit from government action in the form of government spending or money printing. Democrats and Republicans alike have come to love their leaders and to worship big brother in their own way.

Going off Bretton Woods caused economic turmoil, but also enabled the United States to create debt with pure paper money. It helped create a financialization of the economy. Business leaders in the US used to be leaders of manufacturing such as Henry Ford and invention like Thomas Edison. Now, they are faceless men working in Wall Street offices creating nothing tangible, but using debt generation and speculation to generate profits with losses socialized by the government. People like Jamie Dimon are now held up as economic heroes on CNBC.

But just as Bretton Woods came to an end due to too much debt, this current monetary system of paper dollar dominance can come to an end too. The result would be financial turmoil that would be like the 1970's on steroids. You would get inflation growth and an explosion in gold and commodity prices. In the 1970's gold went from $35 an ounce to a peak of $887 an ounce. A similar gain in gold from its low around $250 an ounce in 1999 would take gold prices up to well over $6,000 an ounce. Gold and silver bugs would thrive and, of course, make fortunes.

The system is already breaking down, but what would really cause it to come to an end is if people once against lost confidence in the dollar in the international currency markets. They would do that if they began to worry about the size of the growing government debt and its annual budget deficit. We have seen such situations happen twice in Argentina in the past fourteen years and most recently in Greece and Cyprus. Something similar could happen in the United States if the nation entered a full-blown government debt crisis.

In effect, by bailing out Wall Street banks in 2008 and taking on their debts, the US government and the Federal Reserve turned a crisis for Wall Street into a potential government debt crisis that all Americans could have to pay for. But, so far, there has been no government debt crisis even though the debts are growing. When will they matter?

The Congressional Budget Office (CBO) projects that if nothing is done to control the budget deficit then by 2030 the United States will face a frightening current account deficit of over 15%. Historically, when a nation reaches a current account deficit over 5% its runs into a financial crisis. A level of 6% preceded the 2008 stock market crash.

To put it to you another way, in 2009, the net debt of the United States government was $50.7 trillion. This was debt owned by households, corporations, and central banks all over the world. The CBO has projected two scenarios for US debt. In the first scenario, in which Washington takes steps to control the size of debt by cutting spending and raising taxes, the debt held by the public would be at 52% of GDP in 2037. In the second scenario, in which nothing is done, the debt to GDP ratio would reach 199% in the same timeframe.

Such a level would create a fiscal crisis for the United States, because the CBO projects that at that point just the mandatory spending programs for the federal government would exceed its revenue. If government expenses exceed revenue at some point the budget would hit a point of no return, because as debt grows the cost of financing debt grows too thanks to rising interest payment demands. That would mean big trouble.

As of today, there is no sign that either political party is serious about doing anything about this, or that they are willing to work together to find a solution. No one has been able to lead and make the tough decisions. The Republican and Democratic parties gather the support of voters by existing in opposition to one another, but both parties feed off of the campaign donations of corporate sponsors that are dependent on government financing.

Democrats portray themselves as friends of the little people while receiving most of their campaign financing from Wall Street international bankers, such as Goldman Sachs. Meanwhile the neoconservatives in the Republican Party claim to be for smaller government while they push for reckless wars and ever-expanding defense budgets that drive more money into the coffers of the defense contractors, such as Lockheed Martin, who fund them. So, we have a stagnating economy with growing inflation, growing government that snuffs out private capital investment, and the dangerous expansion of government debt. It's a demonic combination.

What the parties offer the party follower is a symbolic identity. By pledging their loyalty to one of the two parties they get to feel like they are a part of a team, but they get nothing of real substance from their pledge. The party leaders do not talk to you and are not going to help you. They serve their own master. You must help yourself. All you have to do is look at the back of a US dollar bill and reject the false enlightenment represented by the pyramid eye symbol printed on to it. The kingdom of God is within you. Gold may not represent spiritual salvation, but it is your financial salvation.

The politicians have failed us and the US seems to be a nation lacking in leaders. Everyone knows there is trouble brewing in the distance. The CBO projections are talked about at times in the media and in the mainstream financial press, but there is something you need to know about them.

They are based on an assumption so flawed that it makes them practically a fraud. The situation is much worse than most people realize. People inside the Federal Reserve though do know. Time is running out. Instead of decades to go we may have only a few years left to go.

In August of 2007, Frederick Mishkin, who had been appointed to the Federal Reserve Board of Governors by Ben Bernanke - the two have been close friends for decades - wrote a report for the Fed that laid out what would happen to the economy if real estate prices in the United States were to drop and what the Federal Reserve should do if it starts to happen.

The paper called for a rapid reduction in interest rates to near zero. The report predicted everything that was to come.

I got a hold of it in September 2007, and after I read it I realized that the US economy and stock market were in big trouble. With this knowledge, I actually bet against the stock market in 2008 and made a gain of over 35% in my main account as the stock market crashed and almost everyone else lost tons of money in it.

It was one of the most important papers I have read in my life, and as soon as I read it I shared it with all of the people I could on my WallStreetWindow website.

Today, Fred Mishkin no longer serves on the Federal Reserve Board, but he and a team of economists presented another paper back in February, 2013, at a Federal Reserve policy conference titled "Crunch Time: Fiscal Crises and the Role of Monetary Policy." In this report they predict another financial crisis in a few years - this time focused on a government funding debt disaster - if nothing is done.

So far, at publication time of this book, no American mainstream reporter has done a story about the report. CNBC has not informed its viewers about it and as far as I can tell there has not been any mention of it even in the Wall Street Journal.

Of course, I do not recall CNBC sharing with their audience the 2007 Mishkin report so it's no surprise that they aren't telling their audience about this one either. Journalists in the United States are asleep and TV news is just propaganda. I can't find a single story about it anywhere. I have a link to the report in a post I did about it on my website. If you want to read the whole thing just type "wallstreetwindow crunch time" in Google search and you can find my post.

Now, despite the seeming press blackout, this was a hot topic of discussion inside the Federal Reserve in 2013. At the end of February 2013, a panel convened at the Fed's "U.S. Monetary Policy Forum" in Chicago to talk just about the report. Mishkin then presented a revised version of the report in August of 2013 at the annual Jackson Hole Fed gathering.

The report begins with an abstract summary of what is to come in the rest of its 94 pages. The summary contains these lines:

> "We analyze the recent experience of advanced economies using both econometric methods and case studies and conclude that countries with debt above 80% of GDP and persistent current-account deficits are vulnerable to a rapid fiscal deterioration as a result of these tipping-point dynamics. Such feedback is left out of current long-term U.S. budget projections and could make it much more difficult for the U.S. to maintain a sustainable budget course. A potential fiscal crunch also puts fundamental limits on what monetary policy is able to achieve. In simulations of the Federal Reserve's balance sheet, we find that under our baseline assumptions, in 2017-18 the Fed will be running sizable income losses on its portfolio net of operating and other expenses and therefore for a time will be unable to make remittances to the U.S. Treasury. Under alternative scenarios that allow for an emergence of fiscal concerns, the Fed's net losses would be more substantial."

The study goes on to look at the history of financial government debt crises in countries all over the world and finds that when the ratio of government debt to GDP passes the 80% mark, eventually some sort of crisis hits. These crisis can hit suddenly when the costs to finance government deficits increases exponentially due to a rise in interest rates. Then governments can no longer manage their debts and must default or print them away. This isn't really new stuff. A great book came out a few years ago, titled This Time Is Different, by a group of economists who studied all of this using historic economic data from countries all over the world and broke down the various ways these debt blow ups tend to play out. This "Crunch Time" report uses this book as a source. It's worth reading too.

Now as I have mentioned, based on CBO projections twenty-five years from now, and sometime around 2030-2037, has been the mainstream target for seeing a future of debt trouble for the United States. In the last chapter of my book The War State (you can find it on Amazon too), I cite a Peter Peterson article in the foreign policy journal Foreign Affairs where he uses these CBOE figures and targets the same time period around 2030 as our window of trouble.

However, once you get to page 47 of the Mishkin "Crunch Time" report, you get to the scary stuff. If you find it on the internet and read it for yourself you'll see that the CBO figures people are using in these projections are based on the faulty assumption that interest rates will stay at their current historically low near zero levels forever. If rates go up than the costs of funding the government debt would suddenly rise exponentially - the government debt to GDP will then skyrocket well above the 100% crisis level overnight. Investors all over the world would demand a higher rate of interest to fund the country's national debt, the dollar would decline, and another economic crisis worse than the one of 2008 would hit the United States as the cost for the federal government and the Federal Reserve to finance the debt escalates.

As this "Crunch Time" report states:

"In 2012, debt service was quite low (less than 1.4% of GDP) because interest rates were so low. Roughly one-quarter of the Treasury debt outstanding is in the bill sector (meaning an original maturity of 1 year or less) and borrowing costs at the short end of the yield curve have been close to zero for the past several years. Even longer-term notes and bonds issued by the Treasury in recent years have had a very low coupon. But, if the U.S. continues to pile on more debt and if we assume – as CBO (2013) does – a normalization of interest rates over the course of coming years (to roughly 4.0% for 3-month T-bills and 5.2% for 10-year notes), then debt service costs will eventually skyrocket."

To put this in simple terms, if the interest rate on the 10-year Treasury bond were to go to over 5.2% than the cost to finance the deficit will explode.

The report states:

"The CBO's baseline estimates (and similar projections produced by the White House Office of

Management and Budget) assume that long-term interest rates rise gradually to reach a level of 5.2% in 2018 and then remain constant at that level despite a continued escalation in the amount of public debt outstanding. The theoretical analysis and historical experience reviewed in Sections 2 and 3 suggest that this assumption could lead to a significant understatement of the potential deterioration in the budget picture because yields are assumed to hold steady at normalized levels as debt continues to accumulate."

The implications of all of this means that the Federal Reserve cannot allow the interest rate on the 10-year Treasury bond to rise beyond 5.2%. To prevent that it would have to increase its so-called "quantitative easing" bond buying program or come up with another one with a new name and purchase more bonds if rates start to rise. The report calls this policy "fiscal dominance" and a way to manage the mushrooming debt "through inflation."

The report explains:

"To see how this would play out in practice, we need to recognize that fiscal dominance puts a central bank between a rock and a hard place. If the central bank does not monetize the debt, then interest rates on the government debt will rise sharply, causing the economy to contract. Indeed, without monetization, fiscal dominance may result in the government defaulting on its debt, which would lead to a severe financial disruption, producing an even more severe economic contraction. Hence, the central bank will in effect have little choice and will be forced to purchase the government debt and monetize it, eventually leading to a surge in inflation."

All of this means that the Federal Reserve cannot allow interest rates for the ten year Treasury bond to go above 5.2%. In order to prevent rates going over 5.2%, the Fed would have to print money like mad if they approached that level. The implications are that we face inflationary pressures, a falling dollar, and the potential for a new crisis by 2018. It would be a historic turning point just like Nixon taking the dollar off the gold standard in 1971 proved to be.

Such an event could mark the final chapter of the era of US dollar global supremacy. It is an era that began after World War II and was backed by the fact that the US dollar became the reserve currency of the world. It has enabled the federal government to essentially run gigantic deficits to fund its military-industrial complex and various social programs.

For investors, the result would be financial turmoil in the stock markets all over the world, and particularly in the United States. You can expect to see the DOW and S&P 500 make some wild swings that wipe a lot of people out. Bonds would not act as a safe haven like they did in 2008. Instead, gold would.

Now you may think all of this is dire and extreme. The fact of the matter is that gold is starting a new bull market and the charts suggest there is tremendous upside to come for gold. Is gold factoring in a dire future to come or just going up in a fun bull market? We cannot be sure, and yes we cannot predict the future.

But, we do not need to. Whatever happens whoever is aligned in the correct big trends will build wealth no matter what happens to everything else. So we just need to know the big trend and the big trend in the markets right now is that we have new bull markets in gold and commodities beginning in front of us that will likely last at least three to five years, because that is the average amount of time a bull market lasts.

In such a scenario the investments aligned correctly to take advantage of such a trend will enable those positioned right to multiply their wealth. And if you are reading this in 2015 you probably still got time to get in the game. Even in 2016 it may not be too late, but the earlier you get in the better. What is the best way to play this trend?

CHAPTER 6

How To Profit From A Gold Bull Market

The safest way to invest in precious metals is simply to buy gold bullion and silver from a reputable precious metals dealer. Then you need to go put them in a safe place that you only tell a few people who need to know. You do not want to just store them in your house! You need someplace secret and safe.

Whether you buy coins or bars is up to you. Most people like a mix of both. I consider my bullion holdings as the safest part of my overall investment portfolio. I think of it as my real Fort Knox.

Inside my brokerage account, I buy gold and silver through exchange traded funds that hold both. I also invest in stocks through such funds too. The symbols of the funds I use are GLD, SLV, GDX, and GDXJ. I am not just a gold bug though. I have bought traditional investments in the US stock market at times and invested in foreign stocks too. There is a time and place for everything.

Although I have been investing in the stock market since the 1990's, starting in 2002 I have been an investor in gold bullion and a trader in gold mining stocks. At the beginning of 2002, I came to conclude that gold and commodities were about to start a big bull market. Since then I have bought and sold out of my positions several times as we have seen several bull and bear markets occur in the gold market since 2002, but at the time of writing this book I believe we are about to see the biggest bull market in gold ever over the next few years.

However, I consider my investments outside of gold bullion to be more speculative in a nature. Mining stocks as a whole tend to be more volatile than gold bullion and can be individually impacted in both positive and negative ways to specific company news. It is not unusual to see gold prices go up and then shares of an individual gold company go down, because it had to announce bad news. It may be a negative earnings release or a need to do a secondary offering to raise money by selling more stock, thereby diluting current shareholders, that hits the stock.

However, the right gold stocks will rise exponentially as the gold bull market continues. Higher risks means the potential for higher rewards.

One good and bad thing about buying gold stocks and exchange traded funds that invest in gold is that you have instant liquidity. If you want to take your investment out all you have to do is call your stock broker and get out at the quoted market price. If you trade online you don't even have to do that. You can just turn on your computer, connect to the internet and type! But easy trades makes it easier to make mistakes.

With gold bullion and coins, you have to find a gold dealer or another individual who is willing to purchase your gold. It's an extra step. If you decide to sell your gold then you have to package your physical gold up and mail it to a dealer or else get in your car and take it to someone.

This can actually be a good thing. Most people who try to trade in and out of gold actually make mistakes. If things go up for a few months they get tempted to sell and then end up left behind when the market goes up without them or else they worry during little corrections and sell on bottoms. So having a nice core Fort Knox position in gold bullion that isn't as easy to sell as pressing a button is good, because it means you'll be less likely to make the mistake of selling out too soon. You'll learn not to worry about it and to just enjoy holding on to it. Most people who own stocks look at the trading quotes all of the time, get stressed out over little gyrations, and mess up.

That said, though, the right gold stocks have the potential to go up even more than the price of gold does over the next few years. You see, the profits that mining companies generate during a gold bull market are tremendous, because when the price of gold moves up their profits explode exponentially. For example, if the price of gold rises from $1,300 to $1,560 an ounce that represents a 20% increase. To show you what this means, right now it costs a gold company on average $1,200 to get an ounce of gold out of the ground. A gold price of $1,300 translates into a profit of $100 at a $1,200 cost. This means that a 20% move in the price of gold from $1,300 to $1,560 translates into an over 500% increase in profits for the gold company.

This gives a gold investor tremendous leverage for his investment dollars and gold stocks tend to rise by a much larger percentage than the price of gold itself during a gold bull market. In fact, the gains can be astronomical, which is what first brought my interest to mining stocks. That should be no surprise because when the profits of a company increase rapidly big stock gains almost always follow.

Mining stocks are essentially leveraged investments in gold and silver. That is why they can go up more than gold does at times and can also crash to nothing too. When the last giant bull market in gold came to an end in 1980, most gold stocks actually went to zero - the companies went bankrupt! After that a few dozen of the biggest companies came to dominate the industry for the next few decades.

The Gold Industry

Back in 2002, when I realized that the opportunities to profit in the gold bull market were going to become a once in a lifetime opportunity that I had to take advantage of, I didn't know anything about gold! I knew a lot about stocks and financial markets, but gold was a whole world unto itself.

So, I realized that I needed to make contacts with gold analysts, newsletter writers, and management teams. I wanted to know what makes the gold community tick so that I could build off of their advice and get access to the private market place. I was determined to make money in gold and decided that I needed to meet and befriend some real gold experts who could bring me up to speed.

So I started to travel to mining industry shows across the United State and Canada. Most of them were organized in the same fashion. They rent out a conference center and divide it up into two sections. In the first section, there are speaker panels and smaller workshops where you can get one-on-one attention. In the second section, there is almost always an exhibition hall with booths.

These booths were made up of brokers, companies making trading software, and small cap companies trying to attract investor interest. Despite the dozen or so major gold conferences a year, in reality the gold community is small.

When I first started attending these conferences, very little money was actually flowing into gold companies, even though the stocks were going higher. The simple fact of the matter is that gold and the gold stocks are only a small segment of the financial world. At the start of 2001, the combined market cap for all publicly traded gold stocks was less than the market cap of Disney.

As I write this, Wall Street is still shunning them. Mainstream investors and CNBC talking heads have not accepted the fact that gold is in a bull market and the last bear market cycle that ended in 2013 has made most small market players skeptical of the start of this new bull market. They still think that the gold rally will fail and are afraid to commit money to it. This is why the small gold companies still use private investors for financing and depend on newsletters and investment conferences for exposure.

On one hand, this is a good thing. You can make contacts with the leaders of the gold industry yourself and most gold companies are very accommodating toward individual investors. This is a virtual impossibility right now in sectors such as technology. You would have a difficult time trying to meet Bill Gates or Larry Ellison at an investment conference, but you can meet Robert McEwen, who helped to build

GoldCorp into a company with a market cap of over $22 billion at a gold conference.

On the other hand, many tiny gold companies are nothing but pieces of paper and their reliance on small newsletter writers for exposure is a sign of their lack of investment merit. In fact, many of them border on being outright frauds.

When I started to go to investment conferences that featured gold companies, I made it a point to have private conversations with the gold CEO's to get a better feel for the industry. I spent one night with one of them on a $3.5 million dollar yacht watching football and drinking beer. Loose lips are more revealing.

I took a liking to this guy and he seemed straight to me. Of course, he believed that gold would go up, but he also warned me that 80% of the small cap exploration companies are "fake." He has a 25-year background in the industry and knows most of the key players. The analysts don't follow the stocks so all you have are newsletter writers. I asked him, "who can the small investors rely on?"

He laughed and said that most of them are bought off with stock. He told me of one or two that were good, but then added, "you need to understand that they need to make a living."

He went on to tell me that when it comes to exploration companies it is all about promotion. His words made comments that I heard from another CEO of a small exploration company earlier that day come to mind. During that previous conversation, with this dude, he made a sly remark to the effect that gold exploration companies are the best companies to run, because the balance sheet doesn't matter.

Earnings do not matter. The CEO of this small exploration company said that people do not know how to value your properties and it is all about its unknown potential and the "psychology" of gold.

The last time I heard CEO's say that their earnings didn't matter was during the internet stock mania of 1999. Those stocks flew and crashed to nothing. When the gold bull is over most of the small cap gold stocks will go back to nothing too. However, before then you will eventually see bunches of new companies appear out of nowhere and have their moment in the sun.

I got the impression from both men that stock promotion is central to the small junior mining and gold exploration stocks. The man on the yacht point blank told me that it is not the shares of companies with the best prospects that go up the most, but the ones with the heaviest promotion that do. The way he put it, if you have good properties and no promotion the stock will lag, but if you have crap properties and heavy promotion it will fly as gold goes higher. And, if you have both good properties and heavy promotion than you can have a rocket.

The easiest way for people to promote a gold stock is to get newsletter writers involved, especially those that specialize in the gold market. They are the people who can directly reach potential investors. Promoters get them involved by allowing them to buy stock at steep discounts on the private market, paying them money, or by simply giving them shares.

One of the most popular ways to promote a stock is to send out mass mail flyers to investors in the mail. These fliers almost always feature a newsletter writer, who supposedly has earned his subscribers unbelievable profits, and a write up for the company that it should go up 1000% or even more. That write up is the real purpose of the mailing. The newsletter writer is just there to give it credibility.

The problem is that more often than not the investor who buys on these mailings is buying in near a top. The promoter, the newsletter writer, and everyone else involved in pumping the stock already got in way before the flier is sent out. After the last sucker gets in the stock almost always goes back down. You see with no earnings or real prospects they have nowhere else to go. It's like the movie "Boiler Room." If you haven't seen it you might enjoy it. It's a good popcorn movie.

Just so you know, I do not engage in any of these promotional activities. I am not paid to promote stocks. In the gold industry, it is rare to find a newsletter writer who isn't involved in this sort of activity. I've even heard of one writer calling the gold companies himself and asking them how much they will pay him to write up their stock! Luckily there are ways that you can determine whether or not a newsletter writer is doing real analysis or is just giving you a sales pitch. And there are, indeed, a few top-notch analysts out there.

There is a simple way to separate the wheat from the chaff. Anyone who recommends a stock must put a disclosure with their recommendation if they already own shares, or were given stock, or paid cash by the company or a third-party. Read the writer's disclaimer very carefully to find this disclosure. If they simply own shares that they bought, that is one thing, but if they are being compensated to promote the stock be very wary of what you are reading, because it is not an unbiased piece of research.

As time goes on, I expect these conflicts of interest to become a big issue. Investor awareness will increase. I just hope that it won't take a scandal for it to start. For now, you must carefully choose which newsletters you follow. Make sure they are being written by real independent analysts and aren't just tout sheets.

I learned from talking to these CEO's that I needed to be careful in what I invest in. I needed to learn for myself what the best way to evaluate a gold or silver company is. I put lots of my own money into work in the market and I want to buy the best stocks, not just ones that are going up because everything else is, or because they are being promoted. If you are going to buy into a basket of gold stocks you should just buy the best ones.

Types of Gold Stocks

The trick is to determine which gold stocks have real potential. The safest gold stocks are the large producing gold companies. Every collection of gold stocks should revolve around a core holding in a few of the largest producers. These companies include AngloGold, Barrick Gold, and Newmont Mining among others. They are the stocks that are the institutional favorites of mutual fund managers. In fact, if the gold bull market continues the way that I expect it will then Newmont will become a must own stock, much like Cisco Systems was in the 1990's. Yes, at the time of this writing I own some of these stocks directly and all of them through gold stock exchange traded funds.

Generally speaking, the higher the potential gain the higher the risk that an investor takes in a stock. Higher returns are available to gold investors from mid-tier producing gold companies that mine anywhere from 100,000 to 1,000,000 ounces of gold a year. These stocks have smaller share floats so it takes less money flowing into the stock to make it go up in value. The companies have at least one producing mine and often own several mines, some of which may have higher production costs and were closed during the last gold bear market. As the price of gold advances, these mines reopen to provide a boost to the company's profits. A lot of these companies end up getting bought out. Bema Gold, Wheaton River, and Cambior were all mid-tier producers who were bought out at huge prices.

Mid-tier mining companies can become takeover targets and often engage in gold exploration activities. Often, they join smaller exploration companies in developing potential mines. Mid-tier mining companies are very dependent on the price of gold and often take on debt to develop mining properties. As a result, if the gold price drops they often have to scramble to raise more capital, which means diluting shareholders or floating more debt, and some of them often become insolvent during gold bear markets.

Below the large and mid-tier producers are exploration and junior mining companies, which make up most of the gold companies on the exchanges. Exploration companies consist of only a couple of employees, most of whom are geologists, who search for new gold deposits in hopes of finding the next big discovery. They raise money to purchase claims on properties. Their shares are penny stocks and are akin to lottery tickets. Only one in a thousand pay off in the end. Of course the reward when one of these companies hits pay dirt is enormous, but for every one of these stocks that become big winners hundreds become zeros.

Junior mining companies try to transform exploration properties into producing mines. Some junior mining companies have mines in production, but most of them are only a step above exploration companies. Those that do have mines usually have ones of a lower quality and need to open new ones to replace them when they run out of ore. However, when a new mine comes on line into production, earnings for these companies go through the roof.

Both the exploration and junior mining sectors are riddled with stock promoters and are high-risk speculations. There is a reason why penny stocks are worth only pennies. The difference between investing in a bar of bullion and investing in a penny stock is miles apart. There are no penny stocks in Fort Knox.

Choosing Gold Companies as Investments

When it comes to gold stocks, I invest in a core position of large producers through a gold mining stock ETF, such as GDX or GDXJ, which owns a swath of gold producers. Then, I build the rest of my gold stock portfolio around a basket of individual stocks in large and mid-tier producers or emerging producers. I believe they give me a good risk to reward ratio for each dollar I spend, since many of the shares of mid-tier companies double during rallies in the gold bull market. Most of them also trade over 1,000,000 shares a day. That is enough volume to allow me to build substantial positions and prevent any liquidity problems.

I look for mid-tier companies whose gold production is slated to increase over the next few years, enabling their earnings to grow exponentially even if the price of gold does not rise. They may be planning on reopening mines that have been out of production or have purchased mines from junior gold companies. These stocks often end up being the ones that go up the most in a bull market because of their high earnings growth. If you get into them early, you can even buy their earnings growth at a low valuation and make a bonanza.

In special cases, I invest in junior and exploration companies, but only after a full study of their projects. Most of these companies eventually either get bought out or go out of business. When you become one of their stockholders you become a shareholder and partner in their venture. You are making a bet not only that management can succeed, but that they are on your side and are interested in enhancing shareholder value by building a successful operation and aren't just trying to pad their pockets through stock jobbing. You need to know who the people are behind the company and understand their business model. Do they have properties worth exploring and developing, and will they have the resources to execute?

There are simple questions that you can ask. Whose money is already in the company? How much of the company's financing came from insiders and the management team and how much of it came from brokerage houses and individual investors? Is the management team paying itself in large salaries or do they expect to make money from gains in the share price along with their investors? If they are making stock transactions are they buying or selling shares?

What is the background of the management team? Have they built successful companies before? If they made mistakes in the past were they fooled themselves or did they fool their stockholders? Have the geologists involved in the company made successful discoveries in the past? What type of experience does the chief engineer have?

If you ask these simple questions than you'll invest your money with the top people in the industry. The other thing you need to know is how exploration and junior mining companies develop. This will help you evaluate whether or not an exploration company has a viable property or not and if a junior mining company is going to be able to develop a mine.

How Mining Companies Are Developed

Exploration is the first stage of development. Many exploration companies go to hot areas of the market where gold has already been discovered and mined. At some point in a gold bull market area plays develop and exploration companies appear out of nowhere to play off someone else's success. You need to be wary of a company whose only selling point is the area that it is in.

An exploration team will have its engineers survey its properties. Once they determine that there is likely a solid gold deposit, they will need to raise money in order to prove it. The company then drills holes on the property far apart from each other to get an idea of where the gold may be concentrated.

If the first drill results are successful, the company will carry out another drill test, called an "infill drilling" test. This test consists of drilling new holes in between the first ones in order to get a rough idea of the deposit size and ore grade. The drill results are then taken and the gold deposit is classified. You need to understand the classification system so that you can understand how viable the project is.

A deposit classified as a geological resource is the lowest grade deposit. Gold or silver has been found and a rough estimate has been made of its size and grade based on limited evidence. Further evaluation is needed. This classification is also called inferred, estimated, or drill-indicated. This level of resources has the lowest chance of ever being mined and it is best to stay away from exploration companies that tout such properties.

Most deposits are classified as a possible, probable, or proven reserve. Proven reserves have the highest confidence level and are measured with 50 foot drilling spacing. Probable reserves often use 100 foot drill spacing, while possible reserves use even wider drill spacing.

The Securities and Exchange Commission does not allow companies to include possible reserves when they total their ore reserves. Canada accepts them and allows mining companies to include them with their proven and possible reserves in press releases and shareholder reports. In reality, they are very low-grade properties and should not be counted as strong assets on a company's balance sheet. Be wary of Canadian mining companies whose portfolio is made up primarily of possible reserves.

If the exploration company's survey of a property is promising than it will go the next step, which is a feasibility study. This study further examines and defines the ore reserve and its size, identifies mining methods, estimates capital costs, and projects profitability and return on investment. A feasibility study can take up to three years to complete and once it is finished costs are calculated within a 15% margin. The process of going from exploration to a feasibility survey is what turns exploration companies into junior mining companies.

The next stage of development is the construction of the mine. This can cost a hundred million dollars, which is way more money than junior exploration companies have. If they can't finance the operation themselves than they will try to attract a larger partner to assist in the project or buy them out. If gold is in a bear trend than the project will sit idle until a new bull market in gold begins, a fact that causes many projects to sit in waiting.

The costs and time it takes to get the mine in operation can vary widely. A lot depends on the location of the property and the country that it is in. Stringent environmental laws and bureaucracy can drag out the process and raise costs. Once construction begins and the mine is operational more knowledge about the size and grade of the ore is obtained.

Even though a company that goes from exploration to production can be a bonanza for shareholders, it won't necessarily last. All mines run out of ore eventually and the company will have to find new gold reserves one day, if not at the current mine then at another property. If it doesn't than it will likely go bankrupt.

In the end, exploration and junior resource stocks can make profitable speculations, but they are almost all poor long-term investments. That is why, in the long-run gold, bullion acts as a better core investment position than a pile of penny stocks. Gold bullion is your Fort Knox.

AFTERWORD

As this book goes to the publisher in the first half of September in the year 2015 it has only been a few weeks since the United States stock market began a new bear market. Due to the valuation level that the last bull market achieved and problems with the national debt and interest rate policies this bear market is likely to be very dramatic, swift, and destructive to people who stay fully invested in the United States stock market.

However, all bear markets bring incredible opportunities to those that recognize what is happening and adapt and adjust to the new financial circumstances. As this bear market plays out I will spend a lot of time in my Power Investor group looking for ways to bet against the stock market and finding stocks to bet against through short selling and options trades. Nonetheless, some of the best opportunities will be to go long in asset classes, markets, and sectors that will break away from the underlying bear trend of the global stock markets and go into new bull markets on their own.

At time of publication nothing is doing that yet, but gold and precious metals investments have a good chance to do so before this year is over. That is why I spent a lot of time talking about them in this book. But there will be other markets that will do so too.

This book is titled The Stock Market Bubble Bust of 2015 and Beyond, because it is not simply a call of warning for those invested in the United States stock market, but lays out strategies that I plan on using in the coming years to take advantage of the turmoil that the bear market is going to create. So stay tuned to my website WallStreetWindow.com so we can watch how things unfold together.

ACKNOWLEDGEMENTS

Charts in this book courtesy of stockcharts.com. Pictures are courtesy of Wikimedia Commons.

ACKNOWLEDGMENTS

About the Author

Michael Swanson received a Master's Degree in history from the University of Virginia and then dropped out of the college's Ph.D. program to enter the business world. He co-managed a hedge fund from 2003 until 2006 and runs the website wallstreetwindow.com.

Swanson is also the author of the history books Danville, Virginia: and the Coming of the Modern South, and The War State: The Cold War Origins of the Military-Industrial Complex and the Power Elite, 1945-1963, which is also available as an audio book. He is also the author of the investment book Strategic Stock Trading.

You can keep up with his thoughts on the financial markets and get more information by going to his website wallstreetwindow.com and then joining his free email update list.

It is important to let as many people know about the developing bear market as possible in order to help them. Word of mouth is critical for any author to succeed. If you enjoyed this book, please consider leaving a review at Amazon or your favorite book seller, even if it's only a line or two; it can make all of the difference and would be very much appreciated.